Also by Jane Holman

Pearls of Wisdom: For Your Path to Peace

SEEDS OF SELF-CARE

JANE HOLMAN

SEEDS OF SELF-CARE

FOR LOVE AND SERENITY

the kind press

Copyright © 2022 Jane Holman
First published by the kind press, 2022

All rights reserved. No part of this book may be reproduced, stored in a retrieval system or transmitted in any form or by any means, electronic, mechanical photocopying, recording, or otherwise, without written permission from the author and publisher.

This publication contains the opinions and ideas of its author. It is intended to provide helpful and informative material on the subjects addressed in the publication. While the publisher and author have used their best efforts in preparing this book, the material in this book is of the nature of general comment only. It is sold with the understanding that the author and publisher are not engaged in rendering advice or any other kind of personal professional service in the book. In the event that you use any of the information in this book for yourself, the author and the publisher assume no responsibility for your actions.

Cover design: Nada Backovic Designs
Author photo: Julia Matthewson
Editing: Georgia Jordan
Internal design: Nicola Matthews, Nikki Jane Design

Cataloguing-in-Publication entry is available from the National Library Australia.

ISBN: 978-0-6453444-0-0
ISBN: 978-0-6452626-9-8 ebook

For Pete—

You surround me in the power of love.

This book is a love story:
love for self and love for all of life.
Prepare to fall in love.

CONTENTS

Introductory message xiv

Part One
LOVE AND SELF-CARE

Book essence	2
Why now for Seeds of Self-Care	6
My path from pearls to seeds	8
Seeds of self-care inspiration	10
Activating our seeds	11
Self-care and self-worth	12
What is love?	13
What is self-care?	17
The ultimate combination: self-care and self-love	22
Self-care as our warrior against fear: the battle of our lifetime	24
Love and trauma	27
The opposite of self-care and self-love	32
Where is my love?	34
How to access and cultivate love	36

Part Two
DISCOVERING EXTRAORDINARY SELF-CARE AND SERENITY

Dear Reader	42
Sample self-care days	43
Ways to undertake your journey through the seeds	50

THE SEEDS

Affirmations	54
Animals and insects	58
ASMR	62
Art	64
Baths	67
Being popular	69
Body	72
Boundaries	81

*C*andles	85
Change of scenery to enter the unknown	88
Clouds	93
Colour therapy	96
Collective energy forecast	98
*D*ancing	101
Dreams	104
*E*nergy centres	109
Exercise	117
*F*antasy	119
Fashion	123
Feathered friends	127
Feeling free	132
Fireworks	136
Flowers	138
*H*ero's journey	142
*I*f not now, when?	146
Inner peace	150
I've got this, but do I really?	154
*J*ewellery	157
Journalling	159

Kairos time	162
Laughter	165
Letter to your sweet younger self from your higher self	168
Lighten up	172
Money and prosperity	175
Music	181
Nature	184
Netflix and chill … literally	190
No expectations	192
No problem!	194
Oracle cards	198
Outside looking in	203
Past loves	206
Perfume	209
Pets	211
Play	214
Poetry and words	219
Points of view	223
Power	227
Rainbows	234
Reading and research	236
Rising through stories	238

Sanctuary	242
Service	245
Shells	250
Snow	253
Stargazing	255
Stillness and presence	258
Sunsets	261
Support crew	264
Tea	267
The great transition (hormones)	269
Trust	279
Truth	284
Weddings and events	287
Witnessing suffering	290
Worlds within the same world	296
My Personal Love, Care and Happiness Manifesto: A gift from my heart to yours	299
The effects and evidence of your love in bloom	301

Afterword 305

Acknowledgements 308

About the author 310

INTRODUCTORY MESSAGE

Welcome to the next evolution of us; we are in this life together. Would you like to live and be in life in such a way that it becomes self-care and self-love?

My first book, *Pearls of Wisdom: For Your Path to Peace,* was an invitation to embrace a new way of being: functioning in our power and potential through accessing our greatest wisdom and its ensuing peace. *Seeds of Self-Care: For Love and Serenity* arose from the next stage of my expanding consciousness: greater awareness of both self-care and self-love and their incredible power to heal, elevate and transform.

This book is about accessing love through our self-care, which provides the means to care for and nourish ourselves through the ways we receive, observe, connect with, process, and respond to life. I have discovered through self-care that our peace is the foundation for our love. We are more receptive to our inner love when we are calm and present and accessing our parasympathetic nervous system as opposed to its counterpart: the relentless, harmful fight-or-flight mode.

Growing up, many of us were never really taught about finding, seeking or accessing our own inner well of love, nor understanding its power. Love was generally considered something to be felt for another or bestowed on us if we were deemed worthy. We did not know that powerful love was within us all along, just waiting for us to connect with it. Our self-care opens the doorway for healing ourselves, for releasing all that is not love, for revealing what is obscuring our love, for providing the space to feel our own love and for expressing it powerfully in our world.

Seeds of Self-Care: For Love and Serenity is about creating a gateway to greater love and a portal for bringing Heaven closer to Earth. This is achieved through our loving presence, which is facilitated by finally learning to care for ourselves indulgently and in ways not previously recognised or appreciated as self-care. The self-care evident within my seeds of self-care is designed to alter perceptions of self-care—encouraging us to embody our care, and build it into our everyday existence through the way we live, receive and appreciate all of life.

Love is our superpower, and we access it through self-care. No-one else can love us the way we need to be loved to bring forth the best of us. Our inner love has the power to heal anything that stands in the way of our greatest destiny. This book reveals my path for self-care and love to bloom within me and in life: it is not all a bed of roses; sometimes there are lots of thorns to deal with before we can bloom.

Seeds is about accessing a state of being, an approach to living, and a deep caring for ourselves that activates and connects us with great power: our love. This is a love that transforms us and our lives, and it makes us super effective on a planet that desperately needs our greatest potential. The deeper the love we have for ourselves, the more unconditional love we can express for others. This is life-changing and world-changing. Developing a natural proclivity towards self-care and its most faithful companion, self-love, will alter you and your world at the deepest and most life-changing level.

You are here, you are ready. Let's begin the next evolution of you.

Part One

LOVE AND SELF-CARE

BOOK ESSENCE

Love is our birthright, our origin—it makes us feel good and strive to do good. It is the place where miracles and possibility are born. It is not something outside of us, nor is it necessary for it to be given to us by another. It is something that arises from within.

Once love blooms within our internal landscape, it is then drawn towards us from the outside world in beautiful, countless ways. We become magnets for love because that is who we are; like is drawn to like.

We so desperately want love to arise; it is what we have been seeking our whole life, even if unacknowledged. It is the antidote to all that ails and limits us. *Seeds of Self-Care: For Love and Serenity* has arrived in your life, in your hands, to show you the way: such is the power of love.

Self-care is a way to connect with and activate self-love. Self-care takes us out of the mind and into the heart, where healing takes place. Nurture and love yourself, and life will nurture and love you back tenfold.

This book is about love, is for love, and has been guided by love. It is about the power of uncomplicated and perhaps previously unconsidered self-care for healing, transformation, and connection with love. We are moving our understanding of love from the romantic sense towards our awareness of love as something that already exists within us. A love that is waiting to arise more deeply within us through connection with the cosmic universal field of love—a place of magic, possibility, and miraculous transformation and healing.

In *Seeds of Self-Care: For Love and Serenity*, we are activating and connecting with love through our own self-care. Self-care is an act of love towards self: a love that is felt by and impacts all those around us, as we function from our greatest, truest essence.

Self-care is both indicative of and an expression of self-love. Self-care is evidence for self-love: the message you are gifting to yourself is, *I am worthy of nourishing care, now and always.*

The self-care spoken of throughout this book is somewhat beyond the traditional understanding of self-care. This form of care is accessed through witnessing the myriad of ways that life and the gifts that abound around us can help us to nurture, uplift and access love. It is learning to observe and understand deeply that the ordinary can in fact contain the extraordinary—if we are willing to look through the eyes of love and awe. This awareness allows us to become a part of the wondrous and mystical elements of life with deep reverence and gratitude—creating the space for love in action.

May you see, perceive and receive the experience of the extraordinary through the seemingly ordinary.

Within these pages, you will be opened to seeing self-care in a new way: as a sacred act bringing us closer to presence and love. Opportunities for self-care exist everywhere and at any time. All self-care requires is a willingness, our presence, and an openness to receive. It asks that we have the intent to value ourselves enough to seek that which lights us up, nurtures, inspires, uplifts, and fills us with awe and gratitude.

Self-care fuels the elevated emotions that contribute to love—love of self, love of life and love of others. Love is nurturing, caring, kindness, compassion and receiving. If we exist with love as our natural default system, then we exist in the light—and move away from darkness to the space where spirit can enter and help us to move from our human natures into our super natures.

Self-care is a bridge, a doorway to love. The more we love ourselves, the more life loves us right back and mirrors this stance in beautiful, uplifting ways.

If your self-care nourishes you, it is invoking your love.

Self-care and love quieten the ego and keep us aligned with spirit. Self-care shows us and the Universe that we matter, that we are worthy of love; a deep love. We develop a deep reverence for life that we can gift to others.

Look for daily opportunities for self-care, serenity and love to promote healing and wholeness, and to experience greater freedom from our ego and shadow aspects as we connect more fully with our higher selves.

Self-care and love can be found in the ordinary, catapulting us to the extraordinary. This book is about using the gifts of the planet as opportunities for self-care and serenity—and as a pathway to accessing love. It is a triad approach, combining the power of self-care, serenity and love to create a powerful, present life.

So much of what exists on the planet can nurture, calm and empower us—we need to be able to perceive and believe all that is available and possible for us. The energy and opportunity for self-care and serenity is all around us—waiting to gift to us. Are you open to the challenge of receiving on new levels?

On this journey, you will be asked to bring forth new ways of being and seeing and, like me, you will be more than likely 'asked and required' to live this message so that you can positively impact those around you, and encourage them to do the same. I often repeat core messages throughout my writing. This is intentional and for your benefit. We often need to receive information in a myriad of ways before little wedges of awareness can open up our subconscious to embracing new ways of perceiving. Light-bulb moments often occur after we've been exposed to a concept in several contexts over a period of time.

You will find your way to the miraculous through the seemingly ordinary with true presence, awe, appreciation and gratitude—all portals to miracles. Self-care opportunities are in abundance all around us and often require minimal effort or cost. Self-care and self-love are available to all and are not dependent on having a life of privilege, although we must acknowledge that it is far easier for some than others to embrace the great variety of self-care available, particularly in traditional forms. Those of us who are in the position to do so can be generous with our time and resources and work to uplift the hearts and minds of others. When our own cups are full, we can be that powerful!

We need to train ourselves to see and receive the less-than-obvious, often overlooked forms of self-care. Self-care through the unexpected can become our new way of functioning. My challenge has been to seek them out for you; to help forge your path to care and love; to assist you in moving from the complex to the simple when seeking your serenity and love.

Wonder, awe and focus are huge aspects of self-care, as we are taken away from the (often) not-so-nurturing wanderings of the mind and into the present moment, where our power and peace predominate. Savour it all—all the wonder, all the awe, all the captivating moments—to build joy and happiness. Contentment is self-care. Luxuriate in the seemingly ordinary and the simple pleasures of life, which can be created in any moment of any day. It is a choice. Elevated emotions are self-care and love, as they not only enhance our health and wellbeing, but also have the uncanny ability to draw in more to relish and delight in. Create a memory bank of great moments and great experiences to draw on to fuel your living in love.

WHY NOW FOR SEEDS OF SELF-CARE

My first book, *Pearls of Wisdom: For Your Path to Peace,* speaks of facing our emotions, learning from them as our teachers, and then working to release them so we can step into our power and potential. *Pearls* is a great prelude for accessing the path to love. Once we have self-awareness, it is easier to embrace peace and allow this to flow into love. We need to know ourselves, without denial of what is truly going on, and face our wounds and our past to move forward.

Through my own evolution and understanding in creating *Pearls of Wisdom: For Your Path to Peace*, I became aware of the power of love as the next stage of my spiritual consciousness. A strong message in *Pearls* is that the way to our wisdom and peace is through learning from our own responses and reactions to life and from the accompanying emotions. Our emotions are our teachers, revealing what we need to heal to access the wisdom and peace required to open our hearts to love—a deeper love than we have been willing to activate and live through.

Peace within is the foundation for love. Wisdom, peace and love are the ultimate high-vibrational energies that we need to have at the forefront of our lives. Peace implies that we've done the work, we've quietened the ego, we are getting free of self-imposed limitations, we have surrendered, we trust, and we know the Universe has us in its divine hands, and now we get to connect with and be the greatest force in the Universe—love.

We need to do the brave inner work, and have awareness of

how we are functioning and who we are choosing to be. We can then be sparks of the divine and start to see ourselves, others and our paths through the omniscient eyes of love. We get to be leaders, a model for others through the way we conduct ourselves and create our lives. We forgive those who haven't yet awakened to the truth of themselves, and we compassionately accept 'what is' and guide others through our contributions if and when required. We look for commonalities rather than ways to separate and judge.

We can be shooting stars, elevating all those around us by the stardust that trails behind us.

We all desire abundant lives. The state of love brings forth abundance of all kinds: abundance of receiving, great connections, possibility, opportunities and freedom. This book is my path to both abundance and love, as they are one. Love is abundance of all that gives hope and can be cherished.

2020 saw us experience massive initiation, upheaval and discomfort. We were challenged to shed outdated beliefs and ways of seeing, perceiving and believing to make way for a new era—one where love and abundance can seed on our earth with greater depth. By tending to our soil, our seeds can be cultivated into creations of magnificence. From these seeds, we can bloom; we can choose to create a new world of greater connection and oneness—knowing how we are interconnected and a part of emerging oneness.

Life right now is requiring a massive up-levelling, not only on an individual level but also on a global level. Whether we like it or not, our body and soul are calling us to be free of the old limiting ways of functioning. So much is coming up to be healed, to be released.

Extreme self-care and love are required to undertake this emergence into our new selves. Through self-care, we can evolve through our processes of change with grace, meaning and kindness, and step fully into being all we have come here to be and facilitate in the world.

Throughout our change and up-levelling, we need to see and perceive our sameness and have compassion for the journey of others. Forgiveness, respect, and inherently knowing everyone is doing the best they can are essential parts of this. Each person mirrors to us where we are at on the path to love. Whatever we are still in resistance to will be reflected back to us via the responses of others.

MY PATH FROM PEARLS TO SEEDS

I came to realise that the greatest battle I faced this lifetime was with me. I had to free me to find me. I had to acknowledge, own and release my self-imposed limitations. All that was standing in the way of me being everything I came here to be had to go. This allowed me to focus on creating the space to access and be my greatest potential for activating my mission: to first heal myself and then inspire and lead others to do the same. To do this, I learnt about myself through my reactions to life, through my emotional responses, and through that which most triggered me. It was a deep excavation, and it was tough, but I was tougher.

The freedom, the love, and the joy for existence I discovered on the other side of it all was immeasurable, unexpected and life changing. I had to fully embrace all that life was presenting: the joy and triumph alongside the duress and suffering. Both were drawing me closer to freedom and love. I discovered that the world really was my oyster, and I could create many pearls: pearls of success, pearls of abundance, pearls of love, and a life that had previously seemed but a mere dream. Talents and abilities emerged that were beyond my wildest imaginings, and I began showing up in the world with greater strength and a sense of unstoppability.

All along, I had been afraid of my own greatness, as there was a sense of undeservedness and unpreparedness connected with many elements of my life—this came down to a lack of self-love and trust, as this greatness had been temporarily obscured by fear and all its derivatives. Disconnection from love showed up as anxiety and attempts to play small, thus hiding from the world. Doing the inner work and connecting with the love within me and all around me set me free.

Self-care and serenity proved to be the cornerstones of connecting with my love. We open to be and receive love through our peace, not our fear.

Now, dearest reader, you are invited to move from pearls and peace to seeds and love, along with me.

I am so glad you are here and taking this journey with me. You are evolving magnificently and emerging from your cocoon. Our beautiful wings are unfolding to make the world a better place.

SEEDS OF SELF-CARE INSPIRATION

Just as a seed that is nourished by the elements flourishes,
so too can we.
Love and self-care are the nourishment we require to bloom.

I drew inspiration from nature in comparing the power and potential for growth and creation witnessed in blooming as the stimulus for using 'seeds' in the title of this book. We always have seeds growing within us: seeds of wisdom, creativity, healing and love. They may be taking more time than you would like to blossom into your life, but they are there below the surface, waiting to be watered, to flourish and to be cherished by you. We water our seeds with patience, awareness, encouragement, kindness, and celebration of each small sign of growth bursting through the soils of our lives.

ACTIVATING OUR SEEDS

We all have the seeds of our love waiting to take root, bud and burst forth within us. All it takes is our intent, access to our inner guidance and wisdom, and compassionate, loving self-care. Celebrate all growth, no matter how seemingly small, and before you know it, what emerges will change you and your life forever. You will be filled with and surrounded by a love that leads to astonishing creativity, awe, wonder and contentment.

Seeds of Self-care: For Love and Serenity is designed to elevate your emotions to the higher states of wonder, awe, gratitude, nurturing, appreciation, kindness and compassion. These elevated emotional states are ultimately love in action.

Self-care provides a doorway to new living. That is, living in a space of serenity-inducing love: love arising within us and for us; love of others and love for our lives, and all of life.

Serenity is the desired state of being calm, peaceful and untroubled. This is our preferred state—that is, after we have processed emotions that are surfacing for us to acknowledge and release. Serenity is found when we bring awareness to our emotions, and seek to empty our minds of the harmful meanderings and beliefs and instead work to fill our hearts with all that is good on our abundant planet.

Serenity and self-care go hand in hand. Serenity is easily accessible through self-care because we are entering a state of nurturing and focussed attention. We are in a beautifully receptive state, conducive to love. Receiving provides fertile ground for our self-worth and self-love to flourish. Initially, we may be more comfortable giving than receiving. However, receiving is essential for us as it helps to activate greater levels of inner love. Self-care connects us not only to love but also to the powerful present moment. There is joy in our presence and joy is love.

SELF-CARE AND SELF-WORTH

Self-care enhances our self-worth because it is a means for us to gift love to ourselves. Self-worth is the foundation for a great life. It affects all our choices, decisions and reactions. It is the fuel we need to reach for to rocket our dreams into reality. Self-worth helps us to weather the storms and to feel good. When we are feeling good, we are aligned with our higher selves and listening to our inner guide rather than our inner critic. If you too easily shade to pale—that is, play small when your self-worth leads you to feel tiny—connect with love. Ask, what love can I shine on this to elevate and expand?

Self-love arises more freely when our self-worth is strong. The more self-care and self-worth we activate and embrace, the more powerful and effective we are. We have stronger boundaries—that is, we can embrace saying no as required because we are aware of and value what we can and cannot accept, and therefore our energy is less impacted by others. Self-care and self-worth keep our energetic boundaries strong and free of holes.

If we are stressed, burnt out, or resorting to alcohol or drugs, then openings form in our energetic boundaries, making us susceptible to the energies of others. In these states, energies make their way through to us and impact us, rather than being deflected. When our boundaries are strong, not only can we more readily deflect the energies of others, but we can also more effectively radiate love, as we are not buried in the energies that have made their way through to us.

Our boundaries and strength to deflect that which isn't love come from our self-worth. If we are caring for ourselves, we are nurturing our worth and we are plugged into the universal field of love.

WHAT IS LOVE?

'Love isn't an emotion, a behaviour, or even the connection you feel with another person—it's a supercharged, light-drenched, limitless vibrational field of infinite divine energy.'
— Dr Barbara De Angelis

When the idea came through to me that I would be writing a book with the central theme of love, I thought, *Really?* I had always wondered what this love thing was that I would hear of in spiritual circles. It seemed to be some airy-fairy term that did not relate to me in any way. In fact, I actually found it annoying, as I could only grasp the concept in terms of love for another, and my so-called love life back in the day was having a hiatus. What did I know about love? My experience and knowledge of love existed within the traditional parameters of being expressed for others, represented in romance movies, written about in novels, or sent into the airways via beautiful music. It soon dawned on me that I had actually been seeking love and accessing it my whole life—even if, at times, only intermittently. Every time I felt peace and contentment within, I was connecting with love.

What I have discovered is this: when the love that we desire from another isn't forthcoming, we are forced to look within to seek it. So perhaps having an extended period without being in a loving relationship is a blessing in disguise, a rite of passage.

I have definitely been on my L-plates for love for a long time and am still learning every day. I have come to realise it's a choice that can be made every moment through our words, thoughts and actions. I have also found that in making the commitment to take the path of love, life shows up in just the right way to support this growth and way of functioning.

Love is having the courage to let go of fear and all the blocks we have built within us to keep love out. We need to continually reach for feelings of love through whatever means they can be ignited. Self-care rituals, attitudes and experiences are great places to begin.

Love is our potential and greatness; it is our super selves.

Today, I understand that love is all the beautiful elements of life. It is the things we live for:

- Connection
- Abundance
- Alignment
- Personal satisfaction
- Success
- Finding meaning and purpose
- Gratitude

- Compassion
- Nurturing
- Receiving
- Kindness
- Awe and wonder
- Accessing the mystical and the divine
- Receiving guidance in the form of magical signs and symbols

In fact, love is everything that is the opposite of fear—fear being the lower vibrational states and emotions, including doubt, shame, blame, guilt, anger, hate, jealousy, judgement, excessive worry, and revenge. We know we are not in the company of love (that is, we have temporarily lost our connection) if we are experiencing any of these things.

The great news is, it can be easy to re-establish our connection with love. Often, all it requires is a change in our attitude or thought patterns, stepping into gratitude, connecting with the beauty around us (particularly in nature), or indulging in self-care. Self-care always reminds our inner selves that we are worthy of care and love, and it is an integral part of how we be our best selves, not only for us but for those we connect with regularly or fleetingly.

I define love as high vibes and fear as low vibes. If we are feeling the high-vibrational states, then we are feeling love. Love is being in alignment: heart, mind, and spirit. Alignment is being fully connected to our higher selves, our divine connection. We know we are connected when we feel both peace and love. Imagine a beautiful lamp in our home: until it is plugged into its source—although it may look good—it does not shine brightly or work as it should. The same could be said for us.

Love is feeling so good that it permeates every cell in your body.

Love is the healing power of the Universe as lower vibrations are shifted, released, and elevated to new states.

Love is wonder and awe at what life presents.

Love is nature and all her gifts.

Love is the transformer; the alchemist changing all that does not glitter into gold.

Love is deep, deep appreciation and reverence for all of life.

Love is that 'just about to go on a tropical holiday' feeling—an aliveness; the brightness, the anticipation that something amazing is on its way, with a beautiful element of the unknown thrown in.

Love is joy at the simplest elements of beauty—a bird's beak, the sheen of its feathers, the blink of its delicate eye as it takes all of you in—and at the same time takes you to places you didn't know existed within you.

Love is living with possibility as our natural state.

Love is presence—total captivation by a moment or many.

Love is knowing that miracles are our birthright.

Feeling love is about fostering your inner connection to divine energy.

Love is gratitude for all that is and all that is to come, for where we have been and where we are going. We know we are getting somewhere when we choose to place love at the forefront of our existence. As Judith Orloff says, 'Having a firm and persistent belief in the power of love is one of our most enlightened qualities.'

The power of love gifts us the experience of connecting with the power of the Universe. We become living light through love. We can stop searching for 'true love' in the traditional sense. It will find us when we find it within. It can't not find us, because like is drawn to like.

WHAT IS SELF-CARE?

Self-care is a sacred and ever-evolving lifetime journey.

Self-care is soul care. When we care for our inner world, we can flourish.

Self-care is love; it is being able to connect with anything or anyone to invoke our own inner love. Love isn't selective unless we make it so. Caring for and having compassion for ourselves on the good, bad and ugly days is love of self.

Self-care is building fortitude. It is a constant filling of one's cup. It is resilience. It is standing in the light so that when life strikes in ways that momentarily flatten us, we can return the serve and emerge as whole as possible—and maybe even newer and more stunning in our capacity to live and love than before.

For many of us, for a large proportion of our lives we have tended to identify with our mind; to think with our head rather than our heart. Overthinking and identifying with the ego aspects of ourselves has become a natural default system, taking us away from our intuition, peace, power and potential. Self-care helps us to drop back into our bodies and hearts, connecting us back to what nourishes, calms and uplifts us. Self-care leads us into the realm of self-love—that place where we honour ourselves, place ourselves on the top of the pyramid, have strong boundaries and display the best of our courage, purpose, awareness, truth and authenticity.

Our personal power grows through our self-care as we come to know the truth of ourselves, let go of that which no longer serves us, and embrace our greatness. Our personal power opens us more deeply to our self-love. The more powerful we feel, the more we love ourselves. Our personal power brings confidence and inner joy. A state of joy is a state of love.

Many of us experience true joy through our self-care. How can you bring joy into your everyday life through your self-care? What self-care will make you feel nourished and alive?

Paying attention is vital for great self-care, because practising self-care through connecting with and witnessing the seemingly ordinary (but really unbelievably extraordinary) is key. In this space, we discover our super selves through forgetting our ego-controlled limited selves. We can receive love, miracles and abundance when we are free of our self-imposed limitations. Reverently observing all the beauty around us is self-care. Looking around frees us from continuous meaningless thinking as it takes us to the present moment and greater serenity.

I am worth taking time for me is the message that you are gifting yourself through self-care. Self-care means discovering what cares for us; what nourishes and nurtures us and lights us up. Self-care can also give us a sense of adventure, possibility and excitement. We feel love in this space and then we have much to gift to others from a place of wholeness, without the tendency to slip into co-dependence.

> '*Valuing self-care pretty much abolishes co-dependent behaviours, which stem from the unconscious desire to be a hero or martyr.*'
> — Dr Susan Hardwick-Smith

Self-care provides a direct route to abundance, as anything that makes us feel good raises our vibration. High-vibrational states draw in high-vibrational experiences. When we feel good, we keep drawing in more to make us feel good—such is the law of attraction: like loves attracting like. The law of attraction also means we will attract who we are. The more love and positive vibes we emit, the more rich experiences we will draw to ourselves. Part of this is feeling worthy of love and self-care, as this puts our mind, body and spirit on notice that we are worthy of love. When we treasure ourselves more deeply, love cannot help but find its way to us in a myriad of beautiful ways, supporting us on all levels.

Receiving raises our vibration, and we access our ability to receive through self-care. Our self-worth increases through self-care, which further raises our vibration. Self-care plus receiving, plus feeling good, plus self-worth equals abundance!

Self-care makes us powerful, more grounded and centered. We activate our potential because when we are experiencing optimal wellbeing, we feel good. If we're feeling good, we are divinely connected, drawing in abundance of all kinds and accessing our superpowers—those unique to each person. Imagine a world where millions were accessing their superpowers …

Self-care allows us to accept what is going on within and look at ways to shift what no longer serves us. Taking care of ourselves is a powerful and beautiful demonstration of love. It allows us to evolve into our most vibrant, expansive selves. As Dr Wayne Dyer says, 'have a quiet love affair with yourself.'

On your journey through life, embrace the truth that any form of self-care can create presence and lead you closer to feeling good, which is feeling love. Many of us have not actually given ourselves permission to feel good; self-care bypasses the need for permission. Self-care makes us feel good with minimal effort if we are indulging in the forms that are nurturing and uplifting for us. From the space of self-care and the accompanying serenity, life will unfold for us with greater ease and flow. We can let go of the urge to force or control ourselves and our environmental conditions when we realise that controlling is unconsciously resisting love. We can surrender to the magic that is available to us when we release the resistance to love.

Resistance can rear itself in the form of:

- Addiction
- Denying our own happiness and joy
- Over-giving rather than receiving
- Denying our greatness
- Refusing our ability to serve and to make a difference
- Chronic, distracting busyness
- Procrastination
- Giving in to the demands of the ego and listening to its mean voice
- Physical dis-ease and ailments that we focus on to the point where we are too identified with our physical bodies, rather than our spiritual selves
- Defining and identifying ourselves as stressed and using that as an excuse to stay stuck and to relinquish self-care
- Not taking responsibility for our healing, as we've lost trust in our ability to heal and feel hopeless

When we deeply know that we are worthy of care and worthy of love, we are then inspired to bring more to the world because we are so much love. From here, our ego quietens and we get to be love magnets: true forces of light, power and potency. We are in alignment with our higher selves and functioning from the space of love. Self-care helps to fuel us with love, to feel love within ourselves, and to remind us to make choices for love wherever and whenever we can.

How we connect with and love ourselves will be often

mirrored back to us through our relationships with others. The more love we radiate, the better others feel in our presence. We help them to connect with their own love.

Reminding ourselves of how much young children grow and thrive and come alive with love and care can help us to remember the power of love and seek ways to activate it within.

Self-care helps us to activate our best selves: self-awareness, self-worth and self-love. All these 'selves' take us closer to light and love, to living in the present moment, to mindfulness, and to gratitude, appreciation, awe and wonder. As you activate all these selves, you are integrating and bringing yourself together into one powerful, beautiful you and embracing (even if not yet on a fully conscious level) a new way of being, seeing, receiving and perceiving. Being present, transfixed by the moment, is so peaceful as there is no time for anything else. You are bringing Heaven one step closer to Earth and embodying the angelic god or goddess version of you. Let what life is presenting you, what is around you, provide opportunities for self-care and moments to connect with love.

THE ULTIMATE COMBINATION: SELF-CARE AND SELF-LOVE

We are all on a journey back to love and all its beautiful derivatives and emotions: freedom, abundance, power, potential, creativity, peace, gratitude and joy. Our love does not exist outside of us. It is always there, just waiting for us to get free of everything we have put in the way of receiving it. It is unconditional; we are the ones who place conditions on it. Self-care helps us to raise our vibration enough to draw in healing light and love. A deep love will connect us with and draw us to the perfect self-care for us and it will also mean that we know we are worthy of such love and such care. We no longer need to give ourselves permission for self-care; it just becomes a natural extension of the way we live and function. We just need to stay open to receive the limitless possibilities for self-care in the most unexpected places and experiences.

Universe is always drawing us closer to love, and once we are committed to the path, it flows more naturally and readily to us. Optimal wellbeing and care become our daily unwritten intention and life rallies to support and integrate this stance.

Deep self-care means that we do what it takes to create the space and peace and relaxation for us to look within and heal our wounds, hurts and trauma. What we require and desire will vary hour to hour and day to day. We make way for the greatness of us to show up by connecting with love rather than fear. Clearing past issues makes space for new energy and light to come into our being and lives.

Our self-care assists us to explore the relationship we have with ourselves with the purpose of setting ourselves free and functioning with love as our predominant mode. Our love then radiates out to others and inspires them to discover their own forms of self-care: self-care that will take them back to love and to all their associated talents and abilities. From here, we can truly be of service—to our lives and to the lives of others.

Self-care helps us to break cycles of relentless over-giving; to unlearn and release points of view that lead us to believe that receiving and caring for ourselves is selfish. Self-care and love connect us with the greatest versions of ourselves, and from this place of our own overflowing cup, our care and giving are dynamic and transformative and do not deplete us or carry elements of resentment. It becomes reciprocal and simultaneously gives and receives and is fuelled by the power of love. We are connected to source energy and co-create great things; such is the depth of our power and light. Connecting our minds with our hearts places us in alignment with our self-care needs and ignites our divine purpose.

Our self-care allows us to connect with our love and heal ourselves emotionally, mentally, physically and spiritually so we can more fully show up for ourselves and the world. Our power, peace, potential and love are needed not just for ourselves but for the global collective to transition into a new age where the old that no longer serves us is released. Something greater than we can currently imagine is emerging within us, for the world.

SELF-CARE AS OUR WARRIOR AGAINST FEAR: THE BATTLE OF OUR LIFETIME

Fear crushes the immune system and limits our potential.
Replace fear with hope and love.

A powerful aspect of self-care is that it can give us a reprieve from fear—fear that is relentless, stops us in our tracks, removes flow from our lives and disconnects us from our beautiful life force. Comforting and nurturing ourselves in any way lifts us away from fear and towards love. Any movement away from fear is a step forward on the path to love. Any form of love that we can gift to ourselves helps us to heal and transform our wounds into wisdom and peace.

Self-care helps us to be calm and process our fear. It gives us the strength to transmute our fear into action.

Our self-care opens a portal for us to live through our heart space, where love arises. Living through our heart connects us with our heavenly natures. Functioning from our heart space gives us greater freedom from the ego and its ability to move us away from love, into fear. Fear shuts down life and love opens it for us in surprising and beautiful ways.

One of the largest struggles we have in life is with ourselves—it is our most consistent and enduring campaign. We move away from love (high vibes) and into fear (low vibes) in a heartbeat. It is the marathon of a lifetime to continually coach ourselves back to love.

Every time we are triggered, it is an opportunity to learn more about ourselves and work even harder to get free of our personal limiting attributes. These are often modelled off and brought from 'important others' in our lives and from society in general, and/or learned in childhood, so perhaps they are limitations that were never really ours to begin with.

Our fear is usually triggered through comparison, competition, envy, hopelessness and self-doubt. Working through the underlying issues within these low vibrational states provides a great starting point for training ourselves away from fear responses and back into love. I would prefer to put my energy into creating a love-fuelled life rather than feeding my limitations. It's a choice we all get to make moment to moment.

I literally exhausted myself with self-judgement, endless worry, self-doubt and fear over a period of many years to the point I was ready to give it up, as I was so over myself and that way of functioning. I deserved and desired a lighter, gentler way of being, with love at the forefront.

We know our warrior selves are winning the battle against fear when we love ourselves unconditionally—that is, love ourselves fiercely even when things are not going especially well: perhaps when we are tired, unwell, irritated, hurt, sad, anxious or disappointed. If we can connect with our inner well of love and be compassionate and kind to ourselves during adverse times, then we are winning and well along the path to love.

We resist the greatness of ourselves, our light and our love out of fear: fear of having to show up, be seen, contribute and lead in ways we have subconsciously decided are too much for us, or not safe. Stepping into love allows us to shine our true love in this world. A great mantra that I use to free myself of the tendency to slip back into limiting my potential through fear is: 'No resistance to what is, or what is coming. I've got this.' Often, I don't know what it is specifically that I am resisting, but it shows up as anxiety located in either my chest or abdomen. After repeating this mantra over and over, the energy changes and the unease is released. Peace prevails when I step into the place of non-resistance to love and all her expressions.

As it's a free-will universe, we have the choice to function from love (hope, optimism, faith, joy, compassion, trust, peace, eager anticipation, abundance, enthusiasm, passion, contentment and belief) or fear (self-doubt, hopelessness, pessimism, despair, boredom, frustration, irritation, impatience, anger, rage, resentment, revenge, hatred, jealousy, guilt, desperation and hopelessness) in any given moment. We have a choice: what are we going to do with this fear? We can feel it and let it stop us in our tracks, or we can move to release it, transmute it, transcend it and step back into the vibrations of love: trust, flow, alignment, intuition, compassion, and kindness towards ourselves.

We are human and will be regularly triggered to indulge in fear. The great thing is that the more we lean into love through our self-care and spend time dwelling within the elevated emotions, the easier it is to reconnect with love and move away from fear. From here, love can become our natural state and fear just a place we visit every now and then to remind us of why we don't want to be there. It just does not feel good, and we deserve to feel good and draw good to ourselves. Change your emotions one moment at a time to change your energy and change your life.

Open the door to your own courage. It is boundless and timeless. Love will help you to find courage in the face of fear. Your courage will serve you and others in miraculous ways.

LOVE AND TRAUMA

The challenge for all of us who have experienced trauma is to not allow it to destroy us, but instead use it to unlock and bring forth the greatness that such cataclysmic events can unearth. There is the power within us all to overcome all that life presents.

This power needs to be supported by great self-care and great self-love. Connecting with love helps us to (over time) create a newer version of ourselves that is not defined by or identified with the trauma. It helps to create peace, acceptance, forgiveness and enlightenment around the trauma. From here, there is the possibility for it to be transmuted into something new, something less painful.

Connecting with love and our inner strength allows shifts from traumatic stress to growth, new potential and a new reality. We get to become our own hero or heroine in a new story based on love for ourselves and for our next chapter, our next evolution. We can be like the mythological phoenix rising from the ashes, becoming something even more extraordinary.

Trauma is very difficult to release if we are not activating our parasympathetic nervous system through deep self-care. Self-care makes us feel safe and nurtured enough to look within and seek ways of releasing old wounds.

Most of us have experienced trauma and many of us are unaware of its ongoing impact. As decades pass, the old feelings and reactions can become our new normal—we may even believe that we have forgotten or dealt with the trauma as we have become accustomed to how we now feel. We may not be aware that our anxiety, negative thinking, sensitivity to the comments of others, ability to be easily startled, dislike of loud noises, self-doubt, and lack of trust in life and in others can all be aspects of unprocessed trauma. Our trauma responses can open the door to the greatest of our wisdom and healing capacity. We can transform our suffering into awareness and potential, but all healing takes time, lots of time, to move us from fear into the healing power of love.

Along with all the specialist services available, trauma requires extreme self-care to heal. For some, simple things like weighted blankets and yoga soothe the soul enough to provide calming situations for healing to take place. For others, tapping (emotional freedom technique) may be the answer. Perhaps immersion in nature and grounding provide the key. Writing can be a most beneficial form of self-care through unlocking and releasing trauma from our psyche. It may help to process your trauma through journalling—helping to release it from your system and onto the page, one word at a time. I have found meditation and visualisation to be extremely helpful. Take yourself somewhere beautiful in your mind, far away from any trauma triggers. Visualise this place. How does it feel? What can you see? Immerse yourself in the beauty and tranquillity of this place. Draw these feelings and images into every cell in your body and keep them within throughout your day. Take what you can from all the seeds of self-care within this book to help yourself to heal and create yourself anew.

The power to heal is more in our own hands than we may realise.

The experience of trauma is a universal human condition. A

lucky few may have escaped it, but most of us have experienced trauma and traumatic responses to events in life. Everyone's definition of trauma and our responses to it are unique—physical symptoms, unpredictable emotional responses, and flashbacks are common. For many of us, situations and people that trigger painful memories are often unconsciously avoided, which can reduce connection to others and life. Unfortunately, trauma can have a cumulative effect. For example, trauma from childhood that is not processed can lead to anxiety in adulthood as things wanting to be healed and released try to come to the surface. Next, add in life and its potential for more trauma and there are compounded layers that require even more shifting, nurturing and loving.

My own experience of trauma has revealed itself most often through anxiety, viral illness and autoimmune-type responses that are created and then compounded by stress levels and adrenals on overdrive, compromising immune function. My way through has been to acknowledge it, feel it, embrace extreme self-care, and coach myself into believing that all is well and that I am safe and loved. It really requires creating new positive mind stories.

Self-care and love are the ways I have established the right healing conditions for mind, body and spirit. Underneath most trauma are feelings of fear, guilt and shame, and a sense of powerlessness and regret over not being able to fix or change situations we look back on and think we should have been able to avoid. It is what it is, it was what it was, and at the time, it was unavoidable. The first step is forgiveness of self for being in a situation of trauma. All any of us have ever done is the best we could with the skills, tools, awareness and attributes we possessed.

Trauma cracks us open and can let in large volumes of light. Out of suffering comes our greatness when we have done the work and loved and nurtured ourselves enough to move back to wellness. It is not a linear process and requires daily self-care unique to everyone. For me, anything that creates calm in my body—reiki, meditation, nature, water, beauty, positive distraction, awe, wonder and gratitude—has helped to create calm in my mind. Peace is required for trauma to relinquish its grip. Maintaining peace has always been central to my healing.

Trauma healing also requires something greater than ourselves to be most effective: it requires connecting with our higher selves, our wisdom, our intuition, our divine connection. In other words, for our healing to be most effective, we need to connect with our super selves. Connecting with love through our self-care and consequent self-love provides us with a direct route. My go-to has always been to acknowledge what I'm experiencing, feel what I'm feeling and then ask for it all to be surrounded in love and surrendered to my higher power—often! This always lessens the impact, creates greater calm, and allows me to take another step along my healing path. My question has always been, *What self-care do I require today to invoke peace and love for greater healing?* From this question, many of my seeds of self-care were born. I wonder what may come about for you in response to this question.

Love you and your trauma back to wellness through unlimited self-care—as much as you require and desire. Give yourself permission to receive and to feel good. You are worthy and you deserve to feel safe, loved, peaceful and whole.

Miracles, shifts, transformation and increased self-love and self-awareness emerge through the challenging, complex, ever-changing and ever-evolving healing journey. Trauma has broken me down to build me up—and has been great preparation for each new life chapter that has emerged for me. We do not want our trauma to take us away from the energy of equanimity that is the state of calm, of not needing to react to situations or people out of fear or a desire for separation. The challenge with trauma is to keep our hearts open enough to receive the good in life, and to trust and to love. We heal more by staying open to love rather than retreating behind our protective walls. If our walls stay in place too long, they can become armour keeping all of life at bay.

Love can assist us to move away from lack of trust in ourselves and life, overthinking, shutting others out, and doubting our decisions. Take care of you: fuel your body and brain with the right foods and thinking to help them heal and rewire. Step outside of the trauma and allow it some breathing room—some time to shift and change and transform—through meditation and energy healing. Change your story around the trauma: make your new version one that does not portray you as a victim, but a survivor who now chooses to forgive and thrive. This is never easy, but a big life is never easy. It is a great accomplishment, and it can be achieved with healing self-care, patience, and guidance and assistance from amazing programs, modalities and individuals. When we commit to the healing path, it is amazing who and what shows up to assist us—miraculous, even!

We must release ourselves from the impact of our trauma (and from the associated fear and stress viruses) to evolve more fully into love; to be whole and healed. Know deeply within that we expand and grow most when we are tested. The deep, emotionally harrowing work is what frees us after we find relief and new wisdom. We can then lead a dynamic life with all its ebbs and flows.

As we heal, we also heal others, because we lead by example through our own process, journey and growth. Healing our hearts and wounds allows us to drop our protective barriers and more fully allow life (with all its many possibilities and gifts of love) to flow towards us. This is our birthright.

> 'No matter what happens,
> just love yourself while it is happening.
> No matter what you're feeling,
> just love yourself while you are feeling it.'
> — Dr Barbara De Angelis

THE OPPOSITE OF SELF-CARE AND SELF-LOVE

Sometimes, although we would rarely deliberately choose it, it helps us to know what we desire by experiencing its opposite. We come to know intrinsically what does not feel good, which can then help rewire us to seek more of what nourishes us. Each time we indulge in a less-than-ideal state or attribute, and do not feel so good or have a sense of unease, we are provided with just the right contrast and motivation to direct ourselves back to more loving choices, approaches and thought patterns.

When we are not in a state of love, we judge ourselves. We often do not feel worthy of our dreams and desires. We may not trust ourselves to take risks and put ourselves in situations that may be for our highest good.

When out of 'love', we do not flow with life as freely, we compare ourselves unfavourably to others and we give in to lower vibe emotions like doubt and envy. We may feel like a fraud and choose to be less seen and less heard even though, deep down, we know we have something wonderful to offer.

In my experience, the following experiences take us away from self-care and love:

- Judging yourself.
- Getting so fatigued that our energetic boundaries have holes in them, allowing other people's stuff to penetrate.
- Spending time around people who leave us feeling depleted, anxious and unwell—we have 'overstayed'.

- Saying yes when we mean no.
- Avoiding expressing our needs.
- Over-giving and forgetting to fill our own cup up—to the point where we become resentful of others. There is a deep-down, 'When is it my turn?' underlying vibe.
- Wearing so much armour that there is no vulnerability (which is strength and healing in disguise) or letting love in.
- Not honouring you by being the authentic you.
- Overindulging in caffeine or alcohol. This lowers our feel-good vibe once the effects wear off. It is often difficult to maintain feel-good emotions for days after a caffeine or alcohol blowout.
- Consuming unhealthy foods. Over a period of time, this dramatically impacts our emotional, physical and mental wellbeing. We feel energetically and physically sluggish and less than positive.
- Closing off to growth and change.
- Stepping into our superior, 'know-all' personas.
- Listening to the demands of the ego and allowing it to convince us that we are not good enough or worthy of all that we desire.
- Needing to be right, rather than listening to the views of others.
- Speaking over the top of others rather than listening.
- Doing control rather than surrender.
- Disconnecting from our intuition and higher self by allowing the monkey mind to take over.
- Putting others' needs and desires before our own repeatedly; that is, divorcing ourselves and making ourselves less-than—which leads to co-dependence.
- Losing belief in our dreams.
- Avoiding seeking meaning and purpose in our lives.

- Forgetting to be in nature regularly.
- Not following what lights us up on a regular basis.

Just for today, which of these experiences could you seek to be free of? What would feel better for you instead?

WHERE IS MY LOVE?

Love is our birthright. We are all made from and come from the divine—therefore, within us always is our divine spark. Love is already within us and it's what we have been searching for our whole lives in some way. I wish for you a wonderful reunion with your true self, your divine nature.

Even during times of trauma and survival, our inner light is still available to us—it is never extinguished, just obscured by our experiences and most importantly our reactions to them. We can, in any moment, live through love (appreciation, nurturing, receiving, gratitude, joy, peace, contentment, etc.) and release fear. I always remember the common acronym of FEAR (false evidence appearing real) as a reminder to identify when I am in the grips of fear and to move towards lessening its power through whatever means possible. Self-care and self-love are great antidotes for fear and provide formidable foundations for healing.

We attract who and what we are. When your intent is to care for you and heal you—and in so doing, learn to treasure yourself—love will flow into your heart, mind and world and complete you in a plethora of magical ways.

The more love, positivity and joy you emit, the more you will draw to yourself.

'There is a power in your heart far greater than anything you can imagine. This power is your love. It is the limitless, sublime, cosmic life force that pulsates within you, bringing meaning to everything it touches.'
— Dr Barbara De Angelis

We are always searching for love in some way or another, generally through our connections with others or via the things and experiences that we enjoy. We need to seek the experience of love within—through our responses to all that we see, hear, taste, smell and experience.

We are choosing love all the time and may not even recognise it. When the following occurs, we are love in action:

- Every time we don't judge
- Every time we don't need to be right
- Every time we give up control
- Every time we smile at a stranger
- Every time we show kindness
- Every time we are present and listening
- Every time we uplift others with our words
- Every time we keep a confidence
- Every time we recognise the ego at work
- Every time we rephrase a negative thought into a positive thought
- Every time we break free of a conditioned pattern

- Every time we let go of that which no longer serves us
- Every time we create
- Every time we choose not to compare ourselves unfavourably with another
- Every time we contribute in some way to the life of another
- Every time we are grateful for what is
- Every time we care for ourselves by receiving the abundant gifts that planet Earth has to offer: the direct route for love at the epicentre of this book

'Every moment of every day, we are making choices for love. Celebrate the choices you have made for love today …
I grasped the meaning of the greatest secret that human poetry and human thought and belief have to impart: The salvation of man is through love and in love.'
—Viktor Frankl

HOW TO ACCESS AND CULTIVATE LOVE

Knowing how to experience our own love and how to access it are great, life-changing, love-cultivating wisdoms. It's like anything we learn—it takes time, patience, intention, and diligence. It is also important to celebrate small steps that are actually large leaps. Celebrating ourselves is love in action.

Cultivating love within is a unique experience for us all.

Anything that stirs your heart is a great starting point. It might be through noticing love arising within you when you've hugged someone you love, played with your pet or laughed with a beautiful friend over lunch. It may be accessed when you've done something for another that they received joyfully or gratefully. It may be when you've received an exciting surprise or experienced a synchronistic moment or sign. Feel your own vibration of love. It is arising within you. It is not actually coming from anyone or anything—it is radiating outward from you, even though it may have been ignited by someone or some experience. You are connecting with your own love.

The seeds of self-care and tips for your path to love that form the second part of this book are about assisting you to experience your own love: that inner well that is always there, just waiting for you to ignite it. It took me a long time to realise that it was up to me to make the choice consciously and constantly for love. I began to acknowledge that every time I felt good and deliberately cultivated thoughts, emotions, and responses to life that made me feel peaceful or content, I was in fact choosing love. I then started playing with it to see how I could strengthen my responses and broaden my opportunities for igniting love.

We can access our connection to love by being in a state of questioning, and continually asking questions that lead us closer to love.

I started asking questions like:

- How would love respond in this situation?
- What would love do?
- What would this be like or feel like if I added love to it?
- How can I experience love within this situation?
- How can I see and perceive this through love?
- How can I see through eyes of love?
- How can I hear love?

- How can I perceive love?
- If I am living a love-filled life, what would my next action be for the highest good of all?

Being deliberate—combined with the beautiful moments where love would arise within me spontaneously—changed my way of being and living on planet Earth immensely. Consciously choose love in every moment that you possibly can by uplifting yourself and others, and by feeling beautiful emotions within your heart as frequently as possible. Love is elevated emotions, so anything or anyone that makes us feel good is a direct route to love.

One of the highest states of love is found through gratitude. If you feel your state of love 'slipping', gratitude and appreciation will provide you with a direct route back to your love.

We need to return to our true essence—that being receptacles for love. It is easier to access and connect with love than we may have perceived. It may previously have been lost through the distracting 'busyness' of our lives and through the illusions obscuring what is truly love in our lives.

A great way to cultivate love within is by remembering the love that we are. Babies and young children help us to remember. If you are around babies or small children, notice how they radiate love and experience how it is so beautifully infectious. Babies extend love outwards to all they encounter—people, animals and the wonderments of life around them. They haven't yet experienced the wounds and unkind words that cause us to erect walls to protect our hearts from hurt. The problem with these walls is that they also keep love out. We need to work constantly to face our wounds, to feel them, to release them so as they don't lock us into a hardened fortress of our own making. Find the love within to melt these walls.

There is no end point, only unlimited possibilities when we choose to align our hearts and our living with love. This does not mean life will transcend into a bed of ever-blooming roses. We will still have hardships and challenges, as that is the nature of life, but we will learn to love ourselves and what life is presenting to us throughout it all. Our love will ease our duress.

We are only ever given what we can handle and living from our hearts helps us flow and evolve through it all. Old lessons often reappear in life. When we connect to love, we trust ourselves through the process; we deepen our inner wisdom and connection, and move towards greater freedom, peace and power.

Part Two

DISCOVERING EXTRAORDINARY SELF-CARE AND SERENITY

DEAR READER

Celebrating life every day in as many moments as possible is how love can find its way to you. Love will find you in miraculous, unusual and often unexpected ways. All you have to do is stay receptive to receiving it.

I trust my seeds of self-care will open you to your own already-existing and miraculous forms of love. You may find love through a bird, within a flower, through a sunset, in a rainbow or through the magical patterns revealed to you in clouds. It may even be through a compliment from a stranger, the beauty of a dress, or a delicious menu. I hope your days are peppered with 'love miracles' of numerous kinds: those where you focus on the love that is presenting to you, rather than forms that may be currently unavailable—but on the way for you if you believe in them. Be a seeker and observer of love rather than one who resists it or turns their attention away from it.

Congratulations on being the advanced soul that you are for being willing and able to embrace the power of the words within this writing. From here on in, we are working towards getting you to more fully embrace the 'seeds' around you that will support you with your self-care and your journey to love.

The seeds of self-care and tips for your path to love are about assisting you to experience your own love: that inner place that is always there, just waiting for you to ignite it. I hope these seeds of serenity and self-care activate your ability to receive opportunities for experiencing gratitude and embodying the power of your presence. I want you to live in awe, to be mystified by all of life. The self-care seeds will provide wonderful ways for reconnecting with your love—to safely practise dropping your protective walls and at the same time feel what has been within you all along.

My seeds of self-care are the means through which I have cultivated love. I hope they inflame your love too.

The seeds are about learning how to receive and activate the love within ourselves. Even on our darkest days, Universe will provide us with opportunities for light and love if we are willing to perceive and receive its magnitude.

SAMPLE SELF-CARE DAYS

Let's begin with my sample self-care days to open you to more possibilities for incorporating self-care into your life.

Self-care choices and protocols will be highly unique to each person, as what lights up one of us may not do the same for another. Part of getting to know ourselves is finding those experiences and modalities that heal us deeply—restoring optimal wellbeing and passion for living. Listening to and following our intuition will lead us to the self-care that is most desirable for us.

I have my non-negotiables: those experiences and ways of being that ignite my inner well of love. In an ideal world, I would make time for each of these every day. I aim to include all of them over a weekly period. When you are first building self-care into your life, start slowly, without placing unnecessary pressure on yourself in the form of more things added to your to-do list. Even creating self-care experiences for a couple of times a week is a wonderful life-changing pivot.

When you visit the pages of my favourite self-care seeds, you will come to know that opportunities for self-care are everywhere. Often, simple acts of self-care are pleasurable and effective ways to stir the love within that is always there, waiting to arise.

My non-negotiables, even if there are only a few minutes to spare for each in any given day or week, are as follows.

Meditation

I don't get out of bed until I am feeling positive, as my state of mind upon leaving my nightly cocoon impacts the whole day. When life is at its toughest, I need this even more. I am convinced there is more magic, surprises, connection and peace in my day when I meditate before rising.

If I must be up at a certain time, I set my alarm well before I need to leave the bed to allow for this vital preparation.

Exercise

Exercise releases stored-up energy from the emotional body and then clears negativity from the mind. I feel free, clear, powerful, confident, and loved by me after a great workout.

Find exercise that you love doing. For me, overly strenuous exercise belongs more in the punishment category than the self-care one. I choose exercise I enjoy. The powerful endorphins that flood my body place me in the desired state for connection and alignment with love. Exercise is a great reset for mind, body and spirit.

Stillness and silence

I love quieting moments; they restore my equilibrium. These moments often occur with a cup of tea, or via close observation and appreciation of a beautiful view—usually with a treasured book in hand. When at work, particularly on my classroom days, I would make the most of bathroom time to just breathe or coach myself back to positivity when needed. I always cherished small moments being fully present to restore—such as a quick laugh with a colleague or a beautiful comment.

Water

I find water deeply soothing and nourishing. I love the purifying, awakening and invigorating nature of water. I absorb its qualities in my morning recharging shower and in my nightly 'releasing the day' shower. Salt baths are pure access to heaven, chakra cleansing, energy clearing, emotion releasing, thought clearing, grounding and centering. Swimming is my go-to girl—she's been a best friend of mine for a long time—and now she's come into my own backyard. My pool is my nature sanctuary. At rare times of the year (when the Tasmanian climate permits), or if I am blessed enough to be somewhere tropical, an ocean swim is next level.

Wonder, awe and gratitude

I find something to induce the states of wonder, awe and gratitude several times a day, whether it be from a memory, or something I have seen or experienced in real life or via media. I pay attention; I consciously seek to observe wonder and awe and they show up for me regularly.

For example, over fifteen years ago, I had polar bears swim up to me in an aquarium, only centimetres from my face—I can still feel the total awe and wonder I felt at these powerful and beautiful creatures when I recall the memory. Being in a boat surrounded by frolicking dolphins is another flashback that I draw on to cultivate elevated emotions.

These types of emotions are the best form of self-care. We all have these moments to uplift us at any time if we are willing to notice the gifts that are occurring around us. When life is about observation, we never have to miss these incredible treasures.

Great, clean food

In one of life's very powerful contrasts, I had unfortunately not realised the impact that clean, healthy food has on our bodies until my health was compromised. Over a period of six months, I reviewed the whole way I was approaching food—gradually replacing one unhealthy choice for a better one. It was a slow process of detoxing my body and changing habits that had led to decades of less-than-ideal eating patterns. The wonderful surprise for me was not only increased vitality, health and wellness, but also a calmer mind and a more peaceful emotional state.

If I do not eat well over a period of a few days, I not only feel physically sluggish, but a sense of unease also infiltrates my emotional body, allowing my old friend 'worry' to enter my mind in some form or another.

One day, I accidentally put the wrong fuel in my car and was shocked by how little get-up-and-go the car had compared to when it had good fuel flowing within. We are like this too! I thought 'one time' wouldn't make too much difference—I was so wrong. Each time we fuel our bodies, there is either a healing impact or something that our forever hard-working bodies must process at the expense of optimal functioning.

I believe part of our self-care involves tuning into our bodies to work out which fuel works best for us. No two individuals are alike; we each have uniquely different structures, needs, and genetic influences to work with and around.

Nature time

The sounds of birds and bees soothe my soul and flowers elevate me on a mind, body and spirit level. The interesting thing is, the more time I have spent in my garden over the years, the more bees and birds have arrived to make it their home. I am in awe of what I observe and perceive in my garden.

If you do not have a garden, don't ever underestimate the extreme power of a vase of flowers in your home or office. These little beauties will gift to you all day long—the only thing required is your regular gaze and appreciation.

A beautiful and so simple self-care practice for me involves standing on my lawn, grounding my energies deep into the earth, and perceiving the power and gorgeous energy that flows up into my body. From here, I tune into the sounds all around me, feeling more and more elevated and peaceful from moment to moment.

Creative expression

Writing, cooking, putting outfits together and creating beautiful spaces at home are my go-to forms of creativity.

Cooking involves the nurturing of self and others. I am highly present when I cook, as most of the time I 'creatively cook' by intuition, adding in what is going to make my dish delicious. Writing is my fastest route to peace, so not only is it a vocation but also a deep form of self-care. I am in the power of presence and in alignment once I get past some of the things that can get in the way of my writing: namely resistance and questioning *Can I really do this?* I have become very good at addressing these things with practice.

Self-care is about being our greatest supporter and coach when our ego draws us down a rabbit hole that we do not want to be stuck in. Although, once we've 'descended down' a few, we become more adept at resurfacing with style.

Reading

Reading, for me, is self-care for my mind and emotions. I adore self-help books and find the inspiration, increased self-awareness, and light-bulb moments quite joyful and nurturing. Reading takes me into the present moment, as I am absorbed in the material I am engaging with.

Before sleep, I only read fiction novels, particularly fantasy because it takes me away from the day-to-day responsibilities and into the magical realms. Fantasy novels often help generate exciting 'out of this world' dreams.

Reading before bed is also a great sleep inducer. Most nights I seem to end up fighting sleep to finish a page. Reading puts me quickly into a deep, healing, dream-filled sleep.

Sleep

Getting plenty of sleep is a huge priority for me. Everything in my body and life just works better after a good night's sleep.

Throughout nights when sleep is somewhat elusive, I still perceive being in my bed (and just resting) as a form of self-care. Even awake, I enjoy the quiet time with my own thoughts, and I also use my awake time to reflect on all that I am grateful for in that day.

I also find leaving a curtain open and gazing at the stars to be very soothing.

Studies abound on the importance of sleep in our self-care regime due to a myriad of benefits, including reducing stress, maintaining healthy weight, healing, lowering inflammation, boosting our immunity, and effectively releasing emotions from our day.

Contribution, service and work

When I am contributing to my own life or that of another—or providing a service or some kind of inspiration—then I feel fulfilled and purposeful. My life has greater meaning when I am doing work that I feel good about. Finding meaning in our lives is a vital component of self-care.

Expressing love and appreciation for myself, for another person, or for an animal in my life is also a way that I contribute, and also care for and uplift myself. Giving and receiving simultaneously is a beautiful thing.

Beauty

Beauty is love in motion. Perceiving someone or something as beautiful takes us (even if only momentarily) directly to awe, wonder and gratitude—all states I perceive are a part of love.

Lower your threshold for beauty—that is, learn to see beauty in the ordinary and familiar. Beauty arises everywhere if we are willing to perceive it. It does not only exist in grandiose displays, or in other-worldly, often unattainable forms. Beauty may be evident for you in a smile or a facial expression (yes, those wondrous things that have often been deemed unacceptable), or witnessed in the colour and pattern of a ladybird's wings, or in a lilting song lyric, or in the smell and taste of a freshly baked cookie. Perceiving beauty with ALL our senses is self-care.

Observation

Get out of the hamster-wheel head and look around. Distract that beast! Pay attention to what life is presenting today, just for you. Train your mind to be mystified and to fill up with awe. Find meaning in the ordinary to become extraordinary. Feel those neural pathways re-fire and rewire. Before you know it, your mind will be friendlier and far greater to inhabit. It can then work alongside you as a loving, ever-faithful companion for co-creating a meaningful life.

Naturally, at times, life gets in the way of our self-care. We are most likely not going to be able to remember (or have time) to do everything I've mentioned every day. The aim is for progression, not perfection—and most importantly, to work out what works for you. Our self-care needs are as unique as gemstones—and all are beautiful in their own way. Each baby step takes us closer to a life of serenity and love.

This approach to my days is a way of being that has arisen and been cultivated by me over a decade or more. At times, all I might require is an abundance of nature, or I might require a week of regular meditation, or hours absorbed in literature. I 'vary' day to day, as do my self-care needs. Tuning in to what I need is an important component of self-care and a way to express love towards and for me.

WAYS TO UNDERTAKE YOUR JOURNEY THROUGH THE SEEDS

We can find our own pathway to love through our self-care and from the simple beauty that is available in life. We may find our connection with love through the peace in nature, through the serenity of new seeds of self-care and through the abundance of things to enjoy on our gorgeous planet.

So how do we get there? Come take a journey with me as we explore the seeds of serenity and self-care that are the gifts evident in my life. Similar seeds will also be in existence in your life—you may just not have noticed some of them yet. They will appear in a form that will be just perfect for you. All you have to do is notice and connect with what is presenting for you.

William Blake alludes to a way of seeing and responding to our world that is conducive to beautiful living. He says we should, 'see a World in a Grain of Sand and Heaven in a Wild Flower.' Earth is bountiful in gifts. Let me introduce you to the myriad of ways for you to access these miracles and contribute to greater love and serenity in your life. Some of the seeds refer to specific things and experiences as opportunities for self-care. Many of the seeds are designed to reveal that self-care is also about the way in which perceive and respond to life through various scenarios that may be encountered in our living.

Either way, the seeds are about showing you how and where you may activate more possibilities for love and self-care in your life.

It is about how we see, approach and move through life moment to moment, and how willing we are to connect with the wonder and awe that is available to us. Let what life is presenting you, what is around you, provide opportunities for self-care and moments to connect with love.

Throughout this journey, **place how you wish to feel at the forefront of your mind and at the centre of your self-care choices.** Honour your self-care rituals and attitudes as a sacred part of you—that part of you that is in an ever-unfolding state of blooming into more and more love. You are worthy and your love is a superpower that changes the world. Allow your seeds of self-care to unfurl in the perfect way for you to discover even more of you and your love. Do this, and you will open to a new world: a new way of living and receiving love.

You may like to read this section in its entirety. Perhaps you may choose to breathe deeply and connect with the contents page and scan to see which seeds call to you. Your heart and inner wisdom know what you most require and desire. Alternatively, as I recommended in *Pearls of Wisdom: For Your Path to Peace*, you may like to use the book as an oracle—asking questions before opening the book where it feels light and right to do so. If you land on the right page for you, you may experience a shift in energy; a lightness and rightness about the page.

Some questions you may like to ask when using the book as an oracle include:

- Which form of self-care does my soul desire or require today?
- Which seed will allow me to connect with my love today?
- What seed do I require for my highest good moving forward today?
- Which seed would allow me to receive the potential of me?
- Which seed contains a message that is just perfect for me today?
- What form of self-care will help me feel better about myself and my life today?
- What self-care does my body crave today?
- Which seed will help me see me in a new, more positive light?
- What wisdom do I require today as my form of self-care?
- What form of self-care would be most healing for me today?

THE SEEDS

Welcome to the world, your new world,
of seeing, perceiving and receiving the
extraordinary in seemingly ordinary self-care.

AFFIRMATIONS

*Use your mind to empower yourself,
heal your body and connect with love.*

Affirmations are the holy grail of mind and body work and are a quintessential aspect of self-care. Our thoughts condition and program our mind. Affirmations are a powerful tool to recondition our thinking into that which enhances our wellbeing and lives.

These little gems of positivity offer a triad approach. High-vibrational thinking leads to healthy bodies, loving hearts and peaceful minds. Positive, nurturing and uplifting affirmations return us to our power and worth, and therefore connect us with the love we have within.

Upon waking, fill your mind with thoughts that will ignite your day with vibrancy. Upon retiring, reach for calm, nurturing, reassuring thoughts.

Affirmations support our belief system, helping to draw what we desire into our physical reality. We need to embody and believe in what we are affirming, even if what we are affirming may initially feel outside of ourselves and slightly untrue. There is no point thinking positively unless we feel it too. We need to feel as if what we are affirming is already flowing into our existence to make our affirmations especially powerful. When we become the very vibration of what it is we are affirming, our manifestation ability is heightened.

Sometimes we feel like the answers to great emotional, mental, spiritual and physical health lie in all sorts of therapies and modalities outside of ourselves. Taking charge of our thinking by embracing positive affirmations is often so simple that it is not valued. Freedom is created in our minds and affirmations create the doorway to free us of limited thinking that creates limited living. We can teach our brains to create a new reality, one thought at a time. Often, the easiest remedies for healthy mental conditioning—the ones found within—are highly effective.

Affirmations challenge inherited and modelled thought patterns, points of view and ways of seeing and being in this world. So much of what we feel and how we respond to life can be traced back to what we have observed and assimilated from others in our childhood. We were searching for teachers and role models. Unfortunately, our teachers could only model for us their acquired knowledge and skills, and this may not have been serving anyone's highest good. Much of adult life involves unlearning everything that keeps us limited and stuck in old patterns. Affirmations help us to connect with the truth of our inherently positive natures rather than the fearful meanderings of past conditioned responses.

Our physical bodies are deeply affected by our thought patterns. Each thought reverberates out into the world, broadcasting our current status, and each thought is also heard and absorbed by every cell in our bodies. Often, before wellness is possible, we need to convince our bodies that we are healing.

Sourcing books containing positive affirmations or recording our own in a journal surrounds us in light. Being mindful of the thoughts we allow and the words we speak are gifts for self-love. Words contain very powerful vibrations. I understand the power of this phenomenon as many readers commented upon picking up *Pearls of Wisdom: For Your Path to Peace* how light it felt and how uplifted they became when holding it and opening it.

Affirmations lead us back to our true 'kind to us' selves. They make us feel good because they comfort and reassure us. They help us to return ourselves to trusting that 'all is well' and 'we've got this'. High vibe words and thoughts are great coaches for Team 'Us'. We feel empowered as we become the observer and manager of our mind. We relinquish the erratic and non-supportive way the ego manoeuvres our thinking towards worst-case scenarios.

Eventually, with enough reprogramming, positive thinking can become our natural default system. Catch any negative thinking before it gains momentum with comments like *Thanks for sharing, but that's enough for today*.

I find when ego thinking kicks in, it works well to set a time limit. I will allow myself a few minutes to wallow in 'something', and then I am done with that. With purpose and intent, I redirect my thoughts to a more gratitude-inducing and appreciative style of thinking.

When we are positively affirming, we are rewiring our brains and creating ourselves with a little more newness each time we indulge.

Affirmations are such a simple way to move ourselves back into alignment. We raise our vibration and connect with our higher selves.

Mirror work, as written about by Louise Hay, makes our affirmations especially powerful. There is nowhere to hide when we look directly into our own eyes (whilst looking into a mirror) and speak heartfelt words. Initially, this can be very uncomfortable and even confronting as we come 'face to face' with where we are at in terms of our ability to say positive, kind things to ourselves. It becomes easier and more effective with practice! Begin today.

Great self-care begins with how you speak to yourself. Dr Carla Gordon says, 'If someone in your life talked to you the way you talk to yourself, you would have left them long ago.' Give yourself a break by retraining your mind to look at what is right, what is working and what is positive, rather than constantly searching for what needs to be changed to elevate your potential for peace and contentment.

Thoughts create emotions and directly impact how we feel and act. Take the reins of your mind today and trust that if you change your beliefs about yourself, you will transform your life. Changing your thoughts will help you to act in ways that reflect who you really want to be. Let positivity, hope and encouragement be your natural default thinking system.

MESSAGE FOR YOUR PATH TO LOVE

We all have negative thoughts. The trick is to catch them (then they no longer have power over us) and redirect or reframe our thinking towards greater positivity rather than judging ourselves for having them. Judgement of ourselves (and others) moves us away from love. Ask yourself in all situations that are causing concern, 'What is the happiest thought I can think right now?' This question alone can help to retrain how our mind functions.

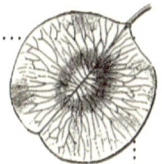

SELF-CARE IDEA FOR TODAY

What can you say to you today, that is exactly what you would love to hear?
Select an affirmation and believe in it deeply. Feel the truth of it within every cell of your mind and body to gain maximum benefit from it.
Say it to yourself throughout the day as often as you can.

ANIMALS AND INSECTS

Every living creature has a unique energy and message for us.

The animal kingdom is a gift from Mother Nature to nurture and guide us. Throughout history, there are stories of heroic acts and great connections with wildlife. In the spiritual world, various animals and insects are thought to convey certain meanings. Many shamans from a range of cultures teach of us each having animal totems that represent what we came to Earth to learn and be, and guide us along our path.

Take notice if there are any animals or insects that are special for you. Do they invoke specific feelings? Do they appear after certain events or during different emotional responses? Many people report seeing butterflies after a loved one has passed over.

The spiritual world often utilises elements of nature to pass messages to us if we are willing to receive such communication. I love the work of Denise Linn. She has a book called *Signposts* that references the symbols and signs that may be evident when encountering many species of the animal kingdom. This may be through certain animals and insects appearing in our dreams, or when they cross our paths, or appear as images either in life or in our minds. I also enjoy using animal oracle card decks to connect with the symbolism and meaning of the natural world.

Our response to each creature is a very personal one. Witnessing whales, for example, either in their natural habitat or via an image, may have a very different emotional response and accompanying message for me than might be the case for another individual.

To develop your ability to connect with the animal kingdom,

learn to be still, quiet, present, and open to receiving information and emotions that may have deep personal messages for you.

Below are some of the messages and experiences I have had through connecting with specific creatures:

- Jaguars—When I see jaguar images, it reminds me to protect my energies and boundaries. I often picture a sleek, black, formidable jaguar prowling my energetic boundaries. I always feel clearer, stronger and protected.
- Ladybirds—Seeing ladybirds always reminds me of abundance and to connect with it and be it. The Universe is unlimited in its capacity to gift to us our heart's desires.
- Dragonflies—These unique little creatures signify magic and possibilities for me and serve as a reminder to embrace the mystical realms.
- Bears—The call to harmonise, to go inward, to restore, to be ready for the thaw and its accompanying new life arises within when I see bear images. They remind me of my own strength.
- Butterflies—These little beauties remind me to be light and carefree and to know that I am free. They also signify connection with the spiritual realms. They are a reassuring sign that all is well and that I am limitation-free. They connect me with my capacity for transformation and are a reminder that I can emerge from my cocoon and be 'brand new' at any time.
- Whales—These powerful creatures remind me of the ancient wisdom and power that is within us all. They seem almost other-worldly, as if they originate from somewhere else in the cosmos and are here to teach us.
- Dolphins—These gentle beings connect me with love, light, kindness, joy and the power of fun, play and connection.

- Bees—Bees remind me to just BE. They teach me of the power of the collective. When we unite and work together with intention, our world is pollinated with blooming life that contributes to all.
- Rabbits—These little creatures, often appearing in storybooks, remind me to be soft, gentle and receptive to life.
- Elephants—These majestic creatures remind me that there is responsibility inherent in having power and strength. True power has elements of grace, respect and awe surrounding it.
- Polar bears—These white marvels are almost otherworldly in their power, purity, strength and presence. Perhaps we could all connect with these qualities to enhance our living.

MESSAGE FOR YOUR PATH TO LOVE

Allow the animal kingdom to gift to you. Learn to receive animal energies and wisdom. We can learn many things about caring for ourselves from Earth's animals. This might be flowing with life and trusting our planet's seasons and cycles. It may be connecting with love through your beautiful responses to animals. You may tap into the level of peace that animals have by just being and accepting what is presented in life. Animals do not resist life; we would enjoy so much more peace and love if we could do the same.

SELF-CARE IDEA FOR TODAY

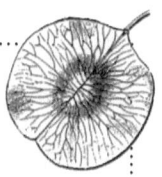

Watch a movie where animals play the starring role or reconnect with some favourite picture books from your childhood that feature animals.

ASMR

Allow your senses to be soothed and your spirit to be nurtured.

ASMR stands for autonomous sensory meridian response. As an extremely brief introduction, it generally refers to the tingly, peaceful feelings that are experienced after listening to certain sounds or descriptions. It often involves soft whispering and what feels like a one-to-one gentle and prescriptive approach. It is delivered in a nurturing way that feels like personal attention—almost as if we might be the only person tuned in. There is much information on the internet if you would like to understand more about the science behind it.

I first heard about ASMR after tuning into a broadcast by two Aussie (larrikin) radio hosts. It was simply hilarious listening to them attempt to imitate YouTube megastar Maria from Gentle Whispering. On behalf of Australia, I apologise, Maria … but they did open the doors to ASMR for it most certainly captured my attention and probably that of many other Aussies too!

I can't pretend to fully understand how it works, but OH, it is such a #soothemysoul experience. After watching an ASMR session, I always feel like I have dropped more fully into my body; I am more grounded, more centered and deeply relaxed.

We are divided in our family in our responses to ASMR—my son and I 'get' it and love it, while some others just laugh and then laugh some more!

ASMR can provide a 'friend' when no one is around to comfort, soothe and nurture you. It is rich in the vibration of love and therefore a great means for us to connect with the love within ourselves. It slows us down, which is vital in our 'let's hustle it and bustle it' world. Its value in creating quieting moments, mindfulness, and brain breaks cannot be underestimated.

Through the ASMR stories, we become extremely present as we are absorbed in the gorgeous episodes. You can be beautifully surrounded by the gentleness and softness of love. My favourites are Gentle Whispering and Whispers Red. Both these beautiful women embrace self-care as a natural part of life. In fact, both have introduced me to other forms of self-care.

There are so many wonderful people in this field, so enjoy exploring and discovering which individuals and styles most resonate with you. It is particularly calming after a stressful day and is quite sleep inducing.

MESSAGE FOR YOUR PATH TO LOVE

Be a self-care pioneer. Explore areas of self-care that may not have been traditionally on the radar. Be guided to the love within via the expert guidance of others. Receive the amazing people advocating new forms of self-care; allow them to take you by the hand and lead you forward.

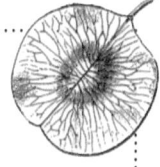

SELF-CARE IDEA FOR TODAY

Type in ASMR on YouTube and treat yourself to a new experience. Let the day drift away and become absorbed in new self-care sensations. Who knows? You may be one of the millions of people on the planet that find ASMR deeply healing, nurturing and comforting.

ART

*Creativity brings light
and love to our lives.*

Art is self-care. Art is therapy. Art is love in bloom. Take yourself back in time to when creating art was an integral part of a carefree, creative childhood. I loved the joy imbued within colouring-in books: a fresh outline for the taking and making. Remember the sensation of first opening a new box of pencils, or the smell, look and texture of a fresh page in a sketchbook. Connect with the vibrant colours and possibilities for creativity and pleasure. Shade and blend the night away!

Give yourself permission to escape the world of adult responsibility and immerse deeply into the magic, wonder and possibility of making art.

Any form of artistic endeavour transports us to the powerful, healing present moment. We are content in this space and generate love within and radiate it outward. Creating something beautiful or something a little crazy lets us explore different aspects of our being. Each time we create something that we value or enjoy, our self-worth grows—love in action.

Through art, emotions and awareness may come forth to help us to grow, evolve and change. Our guard is momentarily down, which makes space for light to flood into our minds and hearts. Moment to moment, we do not quite know what may appear on the page in front of us. Art can teach us about the power and wonder of the unknown—something that our ego tells us to avoid and even fear. When we do or create something we have never done or produced before, we enter the unknown and create ourselves and our minds anew.

Visiting art galleries or viewing great pieces of art connects us with the power and creativity of another being—and with that person's muses and artistic process. Great works arise out of love, even if the original work came about in response to a need to release stuck emotions or suffering. Art is a great healer and transmuter of lower vibe energies. If we tune in with presence and awe, we can perceive and receive the love that went into producing each timeless work.

Art shows us that out of nothing can come something. Unlimited possibilities are for the taking. Creativity is a great antidote for consumerism, as our deep desire for creativity is channelled in a productive way. Our homes become such a nurturing source of creativity as we design spaces with colour, artistic pieces and furnishings that light us up from within.

MESSAGE FOR YOUR PATH TO LOVE

What would it be like if we acknowledged that we ourselves are fine art and created ourselves anew each day? What amazingness and previously uncharted aspects of ourselves could we discover? Love thrives on letting the past be the past, accepting the present and eagerly anticipating unknown future possibilities.
Art creates something brand new and so can we. Proudly connect with your brilliance and love each time you create something new.

SELF-CARE IDEA FOR TODAY

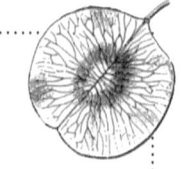

Find images of great works of art. Adopt a meditative, present state and absorb the beauty and the hidden messages that may be there just for you, mysteriously contained within each piece.

BATHS

Warm some water and take a moment to luxuriate and just BE with you.

Baths are an immersion in nurturing and therefore love. When we float in water, we are lighter and brighter. We came into the world surrounded by water, and we are deeply drawn to it as a matter of both survival and 'thrival'. Water sustains life and has long been a symbol of purification. It takes centre stage throughout history and in many creation myths.

Self-care is at its most effortless through the simple act of bathing. The very process of running a bath is a signal for our hearts and minds to let go, flow and just be. There is great joy and healing available when our presence is combined with the sustaining and soothing quality of water. Bathing can become a ritual for cleansing away unwanted energies; especially when combined with Epsom or Himalayan salts. I always bless the water I immerse in to raise its vibration and healing potential.

I love to swim, though a swimming pool has not previously been an easy option. When I take a bath, I visualise myself swimming in all sorts of stunning water environments. Often, I am a beautiful mermaid submerged under the ocean, soaking up the enchantment of the fish; the dazzlingly vibrant coral; the hypnotically swaying seaweed; and the sandy, light-dappled ocean floors. I will even move my arms under the water as if I am performing breaststroke; weird, but most wonderful for me.

The thing is, our mind doesn't often distinguish between truth and reality, so we can make it believe anything if we are willing to feel deeply what we are conjuring and visualising. Self-care involves working with what we can in any given moment. I am a self-care opportunist!

If our self-care lights us up or evokes feelings of comfort and calm, then we are connecting with our love. I delight in regularly taking advantage of the great array of situations and experiences that may not be traditionally considered self-care; those that surround us if we are willing to see and receive them.

MESSAGE FOR YOUR LOVE TO FLOWER

Always use your precious eyes of love to perceive the wonder in unusual opportunities for self-care. Earth and life are plentiful in the gifts offered for those who choose to stay open to and aware of the possibility of their existence.

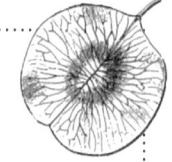

SELF-CARE IDEA FOR TODAY

Take a bath and put your powers of visualisation to the test. Sink back into the warm, calming waters and take yourself off to the most soothing, nurturing and uplifting environment you can imagine. Invite all your senses to participate. What can you see, hear, touch and smell that will be the most caring for you?

BEING POPULAR

*Be true to you and
popular with you, first.*

I think one of the most beautiful acts of self-care and pure evidence of self-love is giving up the need to be popular. From my observations, those who are most insecure and less connected with who they are and where they are heading seem to need large numbers of people around them flowing attention their way and often. Being comfortable having alone time, and even relishing in it, is something we need to give ourselves permission to love and honour if that is what nurtures us.

Looking back on my teen years, I realised that seeking popularity was a safety mechanism. It was born out of fear as opposed to love. There was the underpinning idea that if one didn't fit in, one would be rejected, alone and unworthy. It was much safer to be liked as there would be a flock of others around—safety in numbers, right?

This was one of the many fallacies I had to unlearn in life. Fitting in meant a sameness; a chameleon-like approach to life that didn't encourage stepping up and being my best, most authentic self. It meant seeking the approval of the flock (of sheep) and not deviating too far from what was deemed acceptable. Anyone rising too far above the group would be cut down in some way.

Being popular also had a dangerous edge, as peer pressure led to some unhealthy patterns. Popularity always had a price, and that price often involved partying and excessive drinking, divorcing who I was (to be accepted) and always having a background sense of unease that something was just not right. Attempting to be popular (are we ever really? As it can disappear in a heartbeat) led me further and further away from myself.

Eventually, realising popularity was not in my best interests allowed 'authentic me' to return with greater strength, clarity and wisdom. I definitely got to experience popularity, but it was a double-edged sword that would cut very deeply. It would greatly limit choosing for me and take me away from love, peace, purpose and potential.

Old patterns of seeking popularity can also be triggered and resurface in the workplace if we do not feel safe, secure in our employment or valued for the contribution we make. It can roll into competition and her 'frenemy' counterpart if we don't stay aware and align our behaviour and choices with our true selves.

Fast forward several decades, and I have no need to be popular. It is not appealing as it does not evoke feelings of peace and contentment. My desire to be liked by others has evolved into a desire to be more like me, and this evolves and changes (as it does for you). I associate being popular with too much effort for very little gain or inner reward. I like doing my own thing.

For me, popularity became a trap—a way to limit and contain me. I've realised that being 'me' inspires change and inspiration in others by triggering them and pushing their buttons: kind of the opposite of being popular and instead a powerful agent for change. Being uncomfortable is often what forces us to perceive our limitations and release them. I'm prepared to be this gift for others if all it takes is my true presence … are you?

Being willing to be unpopular set me free to be all of me. Now I am most popular with me and with those that matter most: beautiful souls who are drawn to and love the ever-unfolding authentic me. I am popular with the me who wants to serve and contribute to beautiful and constant change within herself and in the world. This originates from a place of love, not fear. It is accompanied by great care and regard for herself, her journey into the still-unknown aspects of herself, and her path through life.

Your first steps into the realms of self-care and self-love may begin with releasing the need to be liked by many.

MESSAGE FOR YOUR LOVE TO BLOOM

Our connection with others is sacred and vital for optimal health and wellbeing. Focus on the relationships that light you up and allow you to be most authentically you. Quality above quantity: care for yourself by reminding yourself that you are just as valuable if you like a quieter approach to social connection, which includes lots of alone, restorative time.

SELF-CARE IDEA FOR TODAY

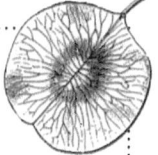

Organise a date with a treasured friend. Being heard is self-care. Laughing with another is self-care. Gifting to another is self-care. Breaking bread with another is self-care.

BODY

*Our body is a supremely intelligent
system designed to support us
for the time of our life.*

Health is our most precious asset. Honour and respect your temple. We must be in control of our own bodies through making the decisions that feel right for us. You are the only one who truly knows what is going on with you. Listening to your body and decoding its language and connecting with your innate wisdom is the journey of a lifetime. Freedom, peace and love exist on the other side of claiming sovereignty over our bodies: this stance is born through our self-care and the accompanying gains in self-awareness.

Our bodies are superbly created to promote our wellbeing and health. They are a part of us, but not us. They respond to every thought and emotion that we have, and at the same time, communicate with us. All we need to do is support the process by maximising our healthy choices on a spiritual, mental, emotional and physical level. We care for our bodies, and they care for us right back.

An essential part of our self-care and self-love is not only care of our bodies but also love for our bodies. They work much better when they are loved, nurtured and pampered as they thrive when our calming, healing parasympathetic nervous system is activated. Our nervous system must be balanced and calm to heal. Stress and the associated high cortisol levels are the antitheses of healing. Harming stress hormones begone!

Our bodies are highly intelligent and know what they are doing. We need to not buy into anything that tells us there is always something 'wrong with us' that only someone else can fix. We have the power and intuition to draw to ourselves those individuals and modalities that can assist with our healing; we also have the answers and the capacity within us to heal what is being called to heal. Our bodily health requires our fierce commitment and fierce awareness of the daily choices we make that may or may not be pro-health. Great food, experiences that light us up, connecting with our higher self to ascertain what is going on within our bodies, movement that we love, and positive thoughts are the fuel our bodies require to thrive. Each 'meal' we imbibe in is an act of either healing and nurturing our bodies, or it is not.

We need to get free of anywhere in our childhood or beyond where we learned helplessness—in the sense that our bodily functioning was out of our control or jurisdiction. We need to move to trust and sovereignty over ourselves and be proactive in our approach to healing our bodies. It is time to reclaim our own power over our health and our healing: this is within us, not outside of us.

We need to develop our ability to tune into what is going on within us that is impacting our bodies. If we learn to listen to the gentle whispers of our bodies, it does not need to scream at us in the form of 'dis-ease'.

My body lets me know when something within me needs to change or requires 'release', as anxiety calls. Anxiety indicates that there is something rising within me that I desire to be free of, or there is something calling that wants to be born through me to help me (and others) that I may be resisting. My experiences—if I listen and act accordingly—then allow me to show others the way, through my way. Listening to our bodies, acknowledging what is required and then taking steps to support our bodies is essential self-care.

Our bodies give our wisdom expression in a physical form: sometimes, our knowing requires a bodily response for it to be fully acknowledged. Your body will show you that if it's not light, it's not love. You will feel the difference in every cell in your body. Return what is not light to sender, with love. Avoid the tendency to allow others to infuse you with their stuff, as it's theirs to heal, not yours. Someone's perceived 'wrongness' does not need to be taken on by you and become your wrongness.

Health conditions can often be gifts, as they make us uncomfortable enough to hear our own truth and to seek love. We need to become curious about what is occurring in our bodies, rather than reactionary. An example of this was when I developed an ear issue. When the ear began to heal, I would lie down of a night and experience this startling, out-of-the-blue whooshing sensation. Suffice to say, it didn't take long for me to go into a state of extreme anxiety over this, sensitive little empath that I am. When I calmed myself down enough to get out of my own way, I started to ask questions around it. The word that came through was homeostasis. When I looked this up, its meaning was around the idea of finding balance. I had to move myself from panic to awe at the ways our bodies heal themselves and perform miracles in every breath we take.

I knew that, somehow, my body was taking care of this ear issue. I embraced the mantra *All is well, and I am well.*

Changing my point of view around various strange bodily experiences (over time) to a state of *What is right about this?*—rather than worrying that there is something wrong—has been very freeing and calming. It is also a great act of self-care and love to trust in the dynamic healing capacity of our bodies.

Every bump and whistle that our bodies make is not necessarily cause for alarm. We can give our bodies time to shift, change, heal, and perform for us without our mind and emotional responses hindering the process.

I have learned that just because I've experienced ill health in the past, doesn't mean I need to go to the worst-case scenario for every bodily sensation I experience. It is about learning to not only trust life, but also our bodies. As my very wise and resilient mum would gently remind me, 'Just relax and breathe, Jane. It's all fine' and 'get on with things.'

We are not our bodies; they are the beautifully designed homes that house us for our lifetime. Care for yours so it can care most effectively for you and then trust it to do its thing. By worrying about various aspects of what our bodies do, we inadvertently work against the very thing we desire most: optimal health and wellbeing.

With the enduring ear condition, I learnt to hear myself—to remove all the blocks, all the stories, all the beliefs that didn't allow me to connect with my soul and my true self, and to be fully me—whatever that looks like, present and future.

Nowadays, it is all about preventive self-care and positive thinking. Health issues have assisted me to get free of believing that anything outside of me has any power or authority over me, and encouraged me to know that I am worthy of all the greatness and abundance and beauty life has to offer.

Issues with our bodies often force us to claim, own, acknowledge and be our power. Reclaim your own body power, your own healing, your own sovereignty—it is within you, not outside of you. It doesn't belong to anyone else. No-one else has the answers for us. Individuals can help shed light and connect us with our own awareness, but ultimately, we need to trust and honour what feels right for us. No two people with the same health condition have the same needs or responses. Our own awareness is found through the profound and consistent self-care that leads to the greatest expression and healing capacity already within us—love.

One of the best forms of self-care I have activated within me is to avoid too much body identification, meaning that every time I experienced something strange within my body, or feelings of malaise, I stopped going to the place of 'something is wrong with me and therefore my life'. I learned to put bodily sensations into a compartment so they didn't define me or stress me.

We are not our bodies. Unfortunately, many of us have conditioned ourselves to think that we are well and happy and on top of things if our bodies are functioning perfectly. The kindest, most caring thing we can do for ourselves is to trust in our body's healing process and give it time to do this without feeling like we have failed, or we are 'ill' in some way.

We as beings are perfectly imperfect, regardless of what our bodies may be experiencing or healing. Aim to keep conditions that require healing in a 'box', so they don't define you or take away your joy if there is dis-ease that needs to be addressed.

Our symptoms and feelings are personal messages from our bodies, about us and for us. We are not victims; we just need to connect with the messages to understand our body's unique form of communication.

If you are like me and have had traumatic bodily or health experiences—for example, losing your sight for three months, as I did—it can take a long, long time and lots of self-care and self-love to regain body trust. This frightening experience was life-changing and opened me to a whole new world of 'seeing' and living, but it did mean for years afterwards that any unexplained health symptoms, no matter how seemingly insignificant, were cause for anxiety. Eventually, I learned to trust my body and feel safe in life again. You can too if you have experienced highly adverse health conditions.

Lean into those you love for support and greater perspective. My husband inadvertently helped me to lighten up about my health and my sensitive, anxious approach to what was occurring with it. I was reeling off a whole heap of symptoms and he was patiently listening as I was getting it all off my chest. I was attempting to make him understand and I said, 'I'd like you to just hop into my body for five minutes just to know what all this stuff feels like for me.' He went very quiet, had a sparkle in his eyes and a mischievous smile, and said, 'There's only one thing I'd like to experience if I was in your body ...' Suffice to say, it stopped me in my tracks, made me laugh and reminded me to just lighten up about it all to facilitate the healing process. Laughter truly is the best medicine, with its high-vibration resonating throughout our body, mind and spirit.

Our bodies love to be nurtured and pampered. It's a symbiotic relationship: what nurtures our body nurtures us, and vice versa. There are countless ways we can pamper our bodies. Yoga, healing touch, and massage are great ways to release unwanted emotions and energies before our adrenals and immune system are impacted. Our bodies respond to our thoughts: peaceful thinking, peaceful body. We feel calm when our bodies are receiving healing, soothing energies and experiences.

Stressing is the opposite of healing. Our bodies are designed to heal us twenty-four seven and do this most effectively when they are not hindered or impacted by immune-system-lowering stress. Stress and the associated overwhelm can negatively affect our decisions and reactions. Stress raises our cortisol levels, taking away our peace, giving us an overactive mind, and limiting our ability to sleep deeply.

Breathing is one of the best things we can do for releasing stress. We need to breathe deeply to cleanse our emotions and allow in love and peace. It only takes three cycles of deep breathing to calm our nervous system. When I am busy, I must consciously remind myself to slow and deepen my breathing.

Self-care is at its simplest through our breathing. We can relax into our body and soothe ourselves by closing our eyes, connecting with our heart (I like to put my hand on my heart) and breathing deeply until calm returns.

Our breathing clears energies and reconnects us to our flow and peace in life. I feel aligned, in flow, and connected with life and my purpose through deep breathing practices. Squeezing all our lower muscles and imagining everything rising and leaving out of the top our head is also very freeing.

Calming our nervous system and activating the parasympathetic nervous system through our breathing relaxes the whole body, which helps us to better digest food and life in general. It's the opposite of fight-or-flight and stress.

When it comes to self-care, our body:

- Desires to be nurtured
- Desires to feel the sun and breeze on its skin
- Desires to be told how beautiful it is
- Desires to move
- Desires to feel the healing power of laughter resonating through every cell
- Desires to hear kind, uplifting thoughts regarding self and others
- Desires to feel the excitement we have for life
- Desires us to process our grief
- Desires us to listen to the wisdom behind our anxiety
- Desires us to release the trauma of our past
- Desires us to become our own healing guru
- Desires us to trust and believe in its innate ability to heal and to know that it is working to heal us twenty-four seven
- Desires us to treat every meal as a healing experience, fuelling it in a way that sets it up to do the best possible work for us
- Desires to be nourished by the energy and the power of nature
- Desires to absorb the power of the ocean and receive the ions that radiate from crashing waves

- Desires to feel our dreams coming to life
- Desires to be fired up via our imagination, passion and dreams
- Desires to be a loving home for us to do our best work on this planet
- Desires homeostasis—balance in all things
- Desires peace and love
- Desires to be healthy: free of toxins and toxic thoughts
- Desires to see through eyes of love
- Desires to hear the symphony of life conducted just for us
- Desires to hear the sounds of birds
- Desires to be held and cherished and desired
- Desires to be adorned in beautiful things
- Desires to sleep in a sanctuary
- Desires to dance
- Desires us to deal with our stress and find a better way of responding to life—flowing and surrendering rather than forcing and controlling
- Desires love to be the dominant theme of our existence

MESSAGE FOR YOUR PATH TO LOVE

Develop your own self-soothing, self-healing toolkit using the seeds that most resonate with you. Take charge of your own nervous system and turn it into a healing system. Do what you can to stay in the high-vibrational states of love—nurturing, peace, kindness, contentment, gratitude and hope—to heal yourself and draw to you the people, situations, experiences, foods, herbs and modalities that will take you on a healing path designed perfectly for you.

SELF-CARE IDEA FOR TODAY

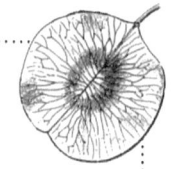

Breathe deeply. Feel and breathe love into your heart and allow that to flow through every cell in your body. Focus on things that induce feelings of love within you to support this process. Concentrate on breathing in light and love and breathing out everything that is not.

If there are things you wish to draw more of into your life, such as joy, trust or ease, concentrate on breathing those things in. The opposite is also true; if there are things you want to release, like fear, anxiety or self-doubt, breathe those out to help you to let go and move forward.

BOUNDARIES

*Strong boundaries allow in what
we desire and deflect the rest.*

Establishing strong boundaries is an essential part of self-care. I particularly like the following fence analogy: farmers need to create great fences to keep what they love in and keep the pests out—and so it is for us. Our self-care builds our self-worth and self-love, which in turn builds strong boundaries. We don't say yes to things unless they feel right and light for us. 'No' is a complete sentence. We don't compromise our own values, needs or integrity to please or gain approval from others, and therefore show others our strong boundaries and make them less likely to be challenged.

Letting people know where we stand helps establish our boundaries and indicate how we like to be treated and what is acceptable and unacceptable for us. We protect our boundaries through the self-care that makes us feel empowered, enhances our self-worth, invokes our power and elevates our presence.

Our boundaries are ever-evolving—they change and develop as we do. We shift our expectations around them with each new relationship, job, connection and awareness. Any time we feel a sense of unease with a particular person or situation, we may need to review our boundaries to restore our inner harmony. Sometimes, all it takes is learning to confidently say no or creating a little time or distance from someone who is difficult for you to be around.

If our boundaries have been impacted, self-care time is vital for restoration. Giving ourselves permission to be and do what we require is an essential aspect of self-care. We have more beautiful energy available to gift love and compassion to others when our boundaries are strong. Finding balance is always key. Strong boundaries help us to be generous with our time and energy without slipping into co-dependent behaviours where we've given our power away to others because we like being needed—or we give up making decisions for ourselves or forget to honour our own needs to please another.

We also need to set boundaries for ourselves—being clear on what we will and will not accept as far as our own attitudes and behaviours go. We may set a time limit on pity parties, judgement, negative thinking, or comparison. Clearing our own toxic energies—accumulated through complaining, blaming, shaming, judging ourselves and others, negative thinking, and holding on to unwanted emotions—is essential for strong boundaries. The thoughts that we allow to infiltrate our minds, bodies, hearts, and energy fields affect our energetic boundaries. Free your spirit of any negative energy; you deserve to feel light and bright.

I had a revelation recently regarding my use of judgement to create boundaries. Before I learned to manage my empath abilities, I had always judged myself for being so 'judgey'. I realised that one of the strategies I used for protecting myself was to keep people who drained me (and their accompanying energies and emotions) at a distance by judging them as not good for me in some way and therefore best avoided. For empaths on overload and those who have not yet mastered their gifts, judgement can be a way to push the world away, to separate, to create an excuse to have one fewer person to deal with (i.e. one fewer person's unprocessed emotions to have to feel or absorb). What I was really doing was attempting to protect my open heart but at the same time inadvertently cutting myself off from many potential relationships and friendships. When we have strong boundaries, we can transmute the emotions of others without having to absorb them and take them on as our own.

Holes are created in our boundaries when we are tired, overwhelmed or stressed. They also form through drug taking and excessive alcohol use. Basically, anything that lowers our vibration weakens our boundaries. Concurrently, anything that raises our vibration strengthens our boundaries. Peace and calm (which are consistently activated through self-care) are high-vibrational states and great friends of our boundaries. Embracing awe, wonder, gratitude and optimism surrounds us with such high vibe energy that our boundaries radiate super strength—like a protective force field. Our joy and our worth are also brilliant for our best boundaries. Valuing you and caring for you creates strong boundaries. Choosing mindfully with whom and where you spend your time impacts our boundaries. Saying no to who and what may be harmful to you supports strong boundaries. Making choices that are in alignment with you and your core desires and purpose equals strong boundaries. Being our authentic selves and expressing our truth creates strong boundaries. Doing what we love daily rather than dishonouring ourselves with work that makes us miserable creates strong energetic states.

Your energy is a precious resource that reflects how you are feeling and how you are responding to and experiencing the world. Our energy fields constantly mingle with those of others, so we need to clear them regularly and shield them to keep our aura strong and clear. Crystals are acknowledged for their ability to protect our energies. Black stones such as black tourmaline, black onyx, and obsidian are renowned for absorbing negative energy. Selenite clears energy and haematite keeps us grounded. Clear quartz is great for keeping you aligned with your higher self. Pyrite is excellent for deflecting negative energies away from you. Rose quartz is most beneficial for keeping your vibration of love high. Crystals are programmable, so give them a job; set them the intention of protecting your energetic boundaries.

MESSAGE FOR YOUR PATH TO LOVE

Having clear boundaries enhances connection and communication because others know where they stand with us and we are free to be our authentic selves and give the best of us. Avoid allowing your boundaries to become armour—we don't want to become so defensive to the world that we block out love and beauty. Listen to your body; it will soon let you know if your boundaries are weakening. You may feel tension in the parts of your body that often call to you most. Always say no when you mean no. Saying yes when that's not what we want to be doing depletes our energy. If we are divorcing ourselves or compromising ourselves to please another, there is always a backlash. We may judge ourselves afterwards or not feel comfortable in our body.

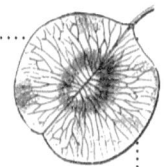

SELF-CARE IDEA FOR TODAY

Cleanse your energetic boundaries by grounding yourself through walking barefoot on the earth, burning some sage, taking a salt bath or an ocean swim, having some reiki or reacquainting yourself with crystals designed to clear negative energies. Protect your energies by surrounding yourself in white light and asking for divine protection.

CANDLES

Candles are reminders of the light that is already within us.

Candles are little gifts of light and love that can form a part of beautiful rituals for self-care, reflection, stillness and meditation. They come in a myriad of forms, showing us that light comes in numerous ways. Candles teach us that there is always light available in the darkness. They remind us to illuminate and release what is no longer serving us.

Candles have always symbolised purity, light and love. They are the ultimate symbol of the joy and light within any celebration. Most festive occasions and dining experiences involve a flickering candle or two. Candles are synonymous with romance; with love for ourselves, and life. We often light candles to honour those who have gone before us. We can also light candles to honour ourselves and the contribution we are making. Let candles serve as a reminder to celebrate all that is worth celebrating within yourself and your life.

Candles are instant mood uplifters and energy transformers. Lighting a candle always brings peaceful energy to a space. Candles in our homes and workspaces elevate the energy of the environments we are in and lift our own vibration. They remind us to connect with our light within.

Part of great self-care is creating peaceful spaces in which to become calm and replenish. Candles invite us to embrace beauty and sensuality with their multitude of colours, textures, presentations and perfumes. Even candle names light me up; I love candles whose beautiful names also signify light, such as Elume and Living Light.

Candles have often been used in sacred rituals to provide us with a symbolic gateway to the higher light realms, and remind us that our earthly life is only a small part of the larger cosmic whole and that there is always a grander scheme of things.

Candles encourage our stillness, our presence, and are therefore great for meditative purposes. They promote feelings of calm and peace, helping us to restore our parasympathetic nervous system and combat stress. Is there anything more relaxing and nurturing than a candlelit bath?

I love this dictionary definition of a candle: *a candle is a unit of luminous intensity*. This definition serves as a reminder that we too have the potential to be beings of luminous intensity. All it takes to light a candle is a spark, and we can provide that spark (and be that spark) at any time. Often, it can be our light, our greatness that we shy away from, as we may have to shine brighter and show up more vibrantly than we are comfortable.

Light a candle and remember:

- You do not have to fear your light
- Your light will set you free
- You don't ever have to extinguish or lessen your light to fit in

To begin, just embrace a steady glow if you are not yet feeling powerful enough to show up with your true vibrancy and luminosity. Each small step, each releasing of some darkness moves us closer to the full spectrum of our light and potential.

MESSAGE FOR YOUR LOVE TO FLOURISH

Allow candles to serve as a reminder to always seek the light within you and all around you. Let lighting a candle prompt you to follow what lights you up to find passion, purpose and meaning in your life.

My life is my work, and my work is my life. I find both are created through love and light—may this be true for you too.

SELF-CARE IDEA FOR TODAY

Light a candle and allow its gentle flickering flame to seduce you into a state of peace and calm. Allow the light of the candle to purify your spirit as you focus on letting go of all that no longer serves your own light. Reflect on and celebrate all that is great and beautiful about you and your life this day.

CHANGE OF SCENERY TO ENTER THE UNKNOWN

Step into the unknown to peep and then leap out of the box.

In recent years, as my children have started creating their own lives, I have been blessed with enjoying greater autonomy over when and where I spend my time. I imagine this is a rite of passage for many parents. Having the cherubs leave the nest certainly cracked open my heart a little (and a lot) on some days. It took some serious reflection and readjustment. The silver lining (as there always is one) is that it also added space for new adventures and insight into what I might like the next chapter of my life to look and feel like.

I started to tune into my own needs and embrace my self-care with greater commitment and awareness. With the spreading of my children's wings and concurrently my own, I learned the value of adding a change of scenery to my self-care inventory. Changing my scenery became such an act of love, as I not only felt amazing, but I *became* more amazing: I was willing to care for me and stretch my thinking and work towards fulfilling my dreams.

A change of scenery creates new thinking, new perspectives, and new ways of being and living.

Experiencing the therapeutic and personally enhancing benefits of a change of scenery doesn't require trekking off to an exotic location, as spending time in a new, previously unexplored local area will suffice. However, time away from one's hometown is most freeing.

I discovered that a change of scenery was a key to presence and mindfulness. I was fully present and engaged in life and what was occurring within me and around me when away from home. As my mind was attending to new sights and experiences, the voice of the ego was quiet and I felt the power of my own presence. All that was not love was quietened. Things had a magical way of flowing, and magic became evident as I entered a heightened, present state. I understood (as per Eckhart Tolle's famous title) the power of now. Temporary relocation was like a personal reset switch. What was currently concerning or worrying me was given a hiatus and a new perspective. Leaving home also allowed me to leave anxiety and worry behind, because when I physically removed myself from current triggers, I was able to rise above these energies and emerge as a newer, clearer me.

Time away gave me the opportunity to think outside the box, because any areas of life that were inside the box had the lid opened on them. I could look from a different vantage point at what I was choosing and creating in life.

Concerns seemed to evaporate as each kilometre of space appeared between me and home life. Time away allowed me to identify where life had kicked into autopilot and routine. Spiritual teachers and psychologists often say that if we keep doing the same things, we get the same results. Trips away allow light and awareness to shine on repetitive patterns and tendencies in a beautiful, non-threatening way.

Changing my scenery always changes my thinking, emotions and outlook, and in so doing, indirectly changes me. Continually observing new things encourages us to 'see' things differently … and to evolve. Fresh ideas and inspiration arise when we are taken out of the current box and into a new creative space. Stepping into an unfamiliar scene of any kind takes us into the unknown, and the unknown is the place from which we grow and awaken. It is the place where unexpected possibilities emerge and where we can witness magic in action.

Doing things for the first time turns us into pioneers creating new frontiers. We create beyond what we have been able to imagine, visualise or perceive as we have the power of the unlimited Universe before us.

I experience greater flow when I enter the space of the unknown, as there is less control and more surrender. Entering the unknown—although it can feel like uncertainty and trepidation, as we do not know what is on the way for us—is the place where possibilities and trust arise. All we can do when entering the unknown is believe within our hearts that only what is for our highest good is on the way to us.

In the unknown, we can receive that which is beyond our own current ability to imagine, perceive or receive. In this space, I feel more alive, more open, more expansive, and more in awe of the workings of the Universe. Nothing is set in stone so there is no sense of smallness, limitation or feeling closed off to what may be available beyond our senses. On the other side of uncertainty is possibility, as we have entered the space of allowing the Universe to do and create for us what we cannot currently do or create for ourselves.

The beautiful unknown is healing and life enhancing. Take yourself there soon.

When I embrace the unknown, it is very much a loving act towards myself as I feel such a lightness, such anticipation, such joy at the possibilities that abound in life. I feel so alive and expansive. I'm not vested in any outcome and feel totally aligned with inner guidance and divine flow. I feel powerful, yet I'm not controlling anything. Heaven on Earth.

When I 'know' everything that is coming, things tend to feel closed off and small. Boredom could be a risk and on the cards.

Motivation and inspiration arise from the unknown because there is no groundhog day in sight. It's called living and loving life.

When entering the unknown, the key is to find balance. We need to work within the constraints of this reality with our jobs, time and responsibilities—but we can always allow space for the unknown to be a beautiful background presence in our lives.

My unknown time is my blank space; my blank canvas on which to create that which hasn't been born through me yet. It is total presence and a break from thinking and feeling. It's stepping into something greater and beyond me. It calms my mind, body and soul and opens me to newness, opportunity and infinite potential. It takes pressure off me—an example of this is when my first book was published. I let my work go out into the unknown. I wasn't vested in outcomes but excited by possibility. I practised trust: trust in the process, trust in my publisher, trust in my intuitive guidance and trust in the Universe to take my book to the places and people it needed to go to.

The unknown leaves energy and possibilities open. This stance also allowed me to be in the perfect space to create the work you are currently reading.

When in flow, it's the unknown from which we draw magic, newness, miracles, opportunities, and possibility beyond what we can imagine. We step outside the box and create new doors to new realities. We change, our energy changes, our environments change, our identities change and our life changes. We are no longer defined by the past and old stories are no longer on repeat. We create from the present and we are connected to all that we are and all that we are yet to become. We are beings of magnitude flowing with love and simultaneously perceiving and receiving love.

> *'How can you know what you're capable of if you don't embrace the unknown?'*
> — Esmeralda Santiago

MESSAGE FOR YOUR PATH TO LOVE

Break routines as often as you can to avoid patterns that may eventually define you. We want to live on the edge of our reality so we can see and feel if there's something more we would like to add. Embrace travel and changes of scenery as a means of dreaming about what comes next without knowing the outcome or having the total picture. Stepping into the unknown encourages us to trust and flow—love in action.

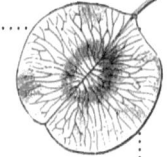

SELF-CARE IDEA FOR TODAY

Change your scenery today to give yourself a reset. Walk or drive to a familiar destination by taking a different route. Have your lunch or cup of tea in a different place. Go to a park or walking track you have never visited. If finances allow, book a trip to a new location. Your body and mind will thank you for it.

CLOUDS

Clouds are reminders that magic transformation is part of our reality.

Clouds are evidence of the randomness and beauty of creation. We can create seemingly from nothing ... from air. The canvas and climate both within and on an outer level can change in a moment. Just as the clouds reshape and evolve into something new, so too can we.

When we step back, observe, relinquish control and just receive, the infinite potential that the Universe has to re-create itself continually is available to us.

Clouds remind us of the power of simplicity: they are just there—we don't have to buy them or demand that they appear. We trust they will arrive in their own good time and be amazing every time. Wouldn't it bring such serenity to our lives if we could trust that amazing things from the beautiful unknown are always on their way for us, and all we have to do is wait patiently and take guided action (sometimes this is as simple as looking up and noticing what is around us) and we will receive? We know something wonderful is coming in its own way, in its own time, and all we need do is notice and receive.

Clouds provide a great analogy for serene living and are an easily accessible form of self-care—all we need do is look skyward and be present and aware. If we watch clouds for long enough, we become so present and so still that, through them, we can hear the whispers of the Universe.

Upon completion of my first book, *Pearls of Wisdom: For Your Path to Peace*, I indulged in some cloud therapy to take a peek at my next possible direction. As I was looking at the clouds and becoming absorbed in their ever-changing patterns, I felt myself connecting with something deeper. My mind became clearer with each passing moment and messages started to come through for me. I distinctly heard, *Three doorways are opening just for you.* As this was occurring, I could see three openings in the clouds. It was my version of the mystical and magical, exponentialized! I perceive that the first 'doorway' was the concept for this book coming through—and it did shortly after. The second doorway was my ability to move from peace to love and at the same time perceive and live the messages of this book. The third doorway was my willingness and ability to show up enough to take my work to the world.

Clouds are ever-changing abstract works of art, synonymous with mysteries unfolding and the unveiling of unknown wonders. They connect us with our own inspiration and creativity as we witness creative design above us. Clouds are creators of awe: an uplifting state that is self-care in and of itself. Clouds tune us into wonder. We are mystified as they morph continually into something new—as we do when we connect with our deep well of love.

MESSAGE FOR YOUR PATH TO LOVE

Clouds are the power of divine creation revealing itself to us in mysterious ways. Connect with this demonstration of love. Allow clouds to mesmerise you and soothe your soul as they beautifully draw you into presence. Feel their calming and freeing energy flooding down upon you. Let clouds remind you to observe, to see, to look up and to remember your spiritual connection and your spiritual self. You are one with all of creation and must therefore be an expression of this cosmic love.

SELF-CARE IDEA FOR TODAY

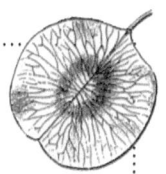

Clouds are a form of self-care and serenity that contains analogies for life and reflection. Tune into the following analogies and messages to see what they evoke within you and enhance awareness of your own wisdom and needs. You may wish to hold one that speaks to you close to your heart today. Breathe deeply before you begin to connect with your higher self.

- Clouds remind us that life is in a constant state of flux, change and contrast
- Just as weather closes in and skies cloud over, so too can life—blue skies always return
- There is always a bigger picture unfolding
- Light is always breaking through
- Embrace the light and shade, the contrasts in life, the unpredictability and the unknown

COLOUR THERAPY

*Life is an assortment of
rich and diverse hues.*

Life is a rainbow of colours. Embrace all the colours of the rainbow. No one is more important than the other, and each serves a different purpose—as it is for us.

Colour is self-care because it affects our mood and our energy. It has the power to uplift and soothe. We live for the green of nature and the blues of the sky. We are purified by the white of snow and uplifted by the yellows of the sun; feel protected by silver and renewed through the rich shades of turquoise. Violet and purple indicate and encourage our connection to something higher than ourselves. Gold reminds us to seek and receive abundance. Jewel tones remind us of the many gems available to us in life. Imagining the pinks in flowers infuses our hearts and minds with love. Orange awakens our creativity and red arouses our passionate sides. Throw on a pair of ruby-red shoes and see how you feel and where life takes you that day. Candy pink reminds us of our playful inner child. Wear yellow if you wish to be noticed, to be seen, to be memorable—or simply to feel light and confident.

Colour is contrasts—just as we are. Our moods are ever-changing colours. Individual colours have been shown to change our emotions. Tune into the colours that you most need today. We have a colour for every vibe within.

There are colours for every season. In winter, with crackling fires, we often like cosy, subdued colours and soft furnishings to snuggle into on colder days. In the summer months, we like to be surrounded by a vast array of vibrant hues—think the colours of summer blooms and bright prints.

MESSAGE FOR YOUR PATH TO LOVE

Allow colour to care for you and raise your vibration. Live a colourful life that excites and inspires you. Never stick to one 'colour'. Variety provides spice to life and opens us to more avenues and opportunities for connecting with and expressing love.

SELF-CARE IDEA FOR TODAY

When you wake up tomorrow morning, ask your body what colour it would like to be adorned with today. You will be surprised how nurtured and cared for your body feels and how your energy is soothed, uplifted or recharged according to what colour you are most drawn to wearing.

The colour that we are most drawn to can often indicate the chakra or energy centre that requires balancing or stimulating for what is coming in our day. For example, if you need to feel grounded, wear red or brown. If you need to be creative, wear orange. If you require calm, wear blue. Your colour choice may very well make you feel better emotionally, mentally and spiritually—especially if you trust your inner guidance to reveal to you the colour you require most on any given day.

COLLECTIVE ENERGY FORECAST

Weather all storms, for they all pass.

I have come to realise (as I have experienced it more deeply since the dawn of COVID) that there is a collective energy we all pick up on: sensitives and empaths will perceive it even more intensely. I seem to receive an 'energetic forecast' each week. Often, clients experience a similar 'theme' playing out in their lives each week as well.

A predominant theme in recent times seems to be feelings of entrapment, which is understandable, considering our experiences of lockdown. This first came to my awareness as, even though I live on an island state where we currently have no lockdown or restrictions and are lucky enough to enjoy our freedom, there was still this entrapment vibe coming through in clients. It demonstrates just how much we are all connected and that what large groups of people are experiencing anywhere in the world has ripple effects that affect us all to varying degrees.

What was particularly interesting was that each client was initially buying into the vibe and creating stories around lack of freedom to try to make sense of it. Unfortunately, they then bought it as real and attempted to make it their own until they could identify the pattern and change their responses. For example, for one client, it was showing up as: 'I'm so over living in my current house. I need a new job. I'm tired of my friends and their dramas. I've lived in this same town too long.' Previously, none of these things was an issue. She (like many of us) was trying to identify why she was feeling the way she was feeling by finding fault in her current life situation. After we discussed this, she was able to release the pattern and refocus her attention on what was working well in her life and what was making her happy. As it turned out, there was a whole lot that she was extremely thankful for: she had been momentarily derailed by the collective energy that was crying out for freedom. The interesting and uncanny thing was that she loved being at home!

There are many themes that come through energetically via the collective. This can be helpful if we tune into what is an overarching theme versus what is true for us. As we are all connected, there is much to learn from perceiving the global energy forecast. It can help us to unearth areas where we still may be limiting ourselves and it can also provide opportunities for us to celebrate how we are functioning and thriving during chaotic, unpredictable times.

When experiencing the collective energy, we can recognise where we may be buying into stuff that is not real for us. This is a great practice for all of life and its diverse experiences. To care for ourselves, all we can do is recognise that a lot of what we are personally feeling is not actually ours and ask our bodies, minds and spirits to release all stored energy and emotions that aren't ours—and do this on repeat.

These times call for exceptional self-care so that we can stay connected to love and keep the collective climate at bay. Our awareness sets us free and allows us to make choices that support us during these challenging times.

There is also much personal wisdom to be gained by bringing consciousness, light and love to the many emotions that surface during tumultuous times. Being free, aware and healthy comes down to our attitudes and points of view. Freedom begins in the mind and lives in the heart. Asking questions about what is going on for us (and journalling our responses) is great for bringing us clarity and for helping us to discern what is ours versus what is the overriding experience of the collective.

MESSAGE FOR YOUR PATH TO LOVE

Choose to feel free and empowered despite what is going on around you. Connect with the love that is within you and all around you—make that your focus when the world seems a little crazy. Find meaning in all that life presents as there is great wisdom and silver linings in every experience.

Be patient. Be kind to yourself and others. Amazing change comes out of chaos, in its own time and in its own way. We can only really be responsible for our inner world and our own responses during these times.

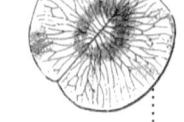

SELF-CARE IDEA FOR TODAY

Connect with your guidance team. Ask questions around what you are feeling.
Is this energy mine? Is this true for me? Is this my emotion or the collective vibe? To all that you perceive is not yours, say 'Return to sender with love and light' over and over until you feel the energy shift.

DANCING

Dance it out to shift it out.

Dancing is self-care because it releases stagnant, unhealed emotions; promotes joy; and enhances our wellbeing on multiple levels. It connects us with our childlike vibrance and freedom from inhibitions. Our daily concerns retreat into the background or vanish completely.

Dancing has great health benefits. It enhances balance, co-ordination and brain functioning when we are attempting to learn choreography. Our bodies love to move and flow. During dancing, we are moving muscles that may not normally come into play and surrendering to the music. Dancing helps to connect us with our sensuality. We feel alive and somewhat more whole after a great dance-off—such is its healing power.

When I was a child, dancing was my happy, creative, magical, 'all is great in the world' place. Unfortunately, when I hit my late teen years, I stopped having formal lessons as the fear of being seen and judged on stage got in the way. Luckily, that little dancer is still in there and I've met up with her again, even if this was long overdue and on a dance floor of my choice, rather than a stage.

If I don't maintain a balance between caring for me versus caring for others, I can unconsciously take on the feelings of others, if I unwillingly take on things for others, or if I play small and attempt to limit myself (and any power that is wishing to flow through me), I can get very adrenal, anxious and headachy, which equates to not very fun. Dancing releases the smallness and the stuff of others and recharges me. I get 'me' back again. The crazier and looser the dancing, the better: this style may require privacy! Sometimes a very lengthy dance-a-thon is required, and at other times a two-song blitz may do the trick.

Dancing reminds us to let go, be free, drop the masks and be all that we are, and to express all that wants to come through us. Most of my stress comes from me trying to not be me; resisting what I'm called to do. The potential of ourselves can be overwhelming. Dancing releases the overwhelm and connects us back to the 'all is well, I've got this, I can and will up-level' state of being and believing. We get back into alignment, love, trust, flow and faith.

I picture a bird flying out of a cage when I've danced and it's a case of *Resistance begone, I'm here to serve* and *What else is possible?* Dancing takes us to the space of demanding more of the great things in life and fewer limitations.

Some more reasons to embrace dancing as part of your self-care and approach to self-love are:

- It reconnects us with, nurtures and honours our inner child like nothing else can.
- It is an antidote for the build-up of stress.
- It clears our energetic boundaries.
- It elevates our emotions.
- It brings us back to the energy of love.
- It demands that we be present. (When one's arms, legs, head and body are going in all directions, it is unwise to be anything but present!)
- It takes us back to the strength of our mind and being.
- It frees us of fear-based emotions and helps to shift and release old hurts and trauma that is coming to the surface, asking to be released.
- It helps us clear unwanted emotions before they become toxic and disease fuelling in the body.
- It causes us to not sweat the small stuff, as we are working up a sweat!

MESSAGE FOR YOUR PATH TO LOVE

Meet up with your little dancer again; you and your life will love you for it. They desperately want you to feel and be free. You've been carrying around that old stuff and those old patterns long enough. You've done the time with past issues and now it's time to let go. Dance it off. When life gets serious, get lighter—dancing shows us the way.

SELF-CARE IDEA FOR TODAY

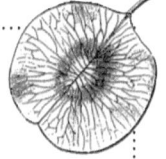

Go back in time and select a song that you loved to dance to at a great stage in your life. Find songs that make you feel free, brave and powerful. Dance in a way that makes you feel light, powerful, and cleansed of unwanted emotions.

DREAMS

Dreams soothe us, awaken our wisdom, and give insight into what we yearn for and can aspire to be.

Dreams are a beautiful form of self-care as they are powerful healing and awakening experiences. They contain stories with hidden meaning of our own existence, allowing us to deepen our understanding of ourselves and the experiences and characters within our lives. They can be prophetic, giving us glimpses into future events. Dreams can also connect us with those we are separated from and loved ones who have passed. Our loved ones can care for us and gift us love from their new home if we are open to receiving this from them.

We need to pay attention to the moods and emotions that our dreams stimulate. Our dreams are often symbolic and contain deeper truths below the surface of what we are observing through our dream lens and perceptions. There are some great dream dictionaries for helping us to interpret our dreams, but I feel dream symbolism is unique to us all and best interpreted personally by us.

Dreams help connect us with our intuition and our inner guidance. In our dream state, our ego is asleep, so we get to perceive things that may elude us in our awakened hours.

Unlocking our own map for successfully navigating our dreams and understanding their messages is fascinating. Practice and intent are key for interpreting the secret world of our dreams.

Record your dreams and insights in a journal (as soon as you wake, when the dream state is still accessible) and you may be amazed at the patterns and observations that are revealed to you about you and your life and where you may be heading over time.

The act of recording our dreams often means they proliferate; we remember them more and can even step into the realm of lucid dreams, where our consciousness runs free.

Lucid dreams are so much fun as we know that we are dreaming and can design them exactly as we desire. Maybe this is how life could be if we stepped into our unlimited and awakened super selves. Just like in lucid dreaming, we could manifest things into our reality with instantaneous ease.

Dreams provide doorways to love and healing. Unpleasant dreams help us to process that which may be too painful to deal with in our waking day-to-day lives. Beautiful dreams fill us with love that flows into our days. Magical dreams flood us with the joy of wonder and awe, and reverence for the mystical and a life of possibility.

I love my dream time; it is so expansive, magical and adventurous. We slip into roles that we may not experience in our day-to-day lives, take risks, succeed in everything we attempt (no matter how impossible or harrowing), heal our wounds, play, and even fly. Time does not exist, and we are free to be totally absorbed in whatever is before us, trusting there is always a way out of even the most challenging of scenarios because we are superheroes. Adopting this super stance in our awakened hours would be great self-care and self-love.

Make 'tomorrow I will remember my dreams' your new before-sleep mantra. Ask your guides and angels to lead you to places of healing in your sleep. Ask questions of yourself around things you would like clarity over before sleep. You may be surprised by what is revealed through your dreams. You may like to pull an oracle card before sleep to meditate on and inspire some guided dreaming. Certain crystals like labradorite, amethyst, blue apatite, bloodstone, kyanite, clear quartz, lapis lazuli and howlite are reputed to enhance dreaming.

I often find I seek to harmonise relationships through my

dreams. Where I've had reactions to people or situations over the years, these scenarios would often play out in my dreams. The dream encounters are generally more positive as I perceive that I am trying to heal or change anything that could have been done with more love and compassion.

In my dreams, I feel that I am responding as a higher version of me. It's like a do-over; a healing chance to rewrite my history with greater elements of love interwoven. My dreams teach me to have compassion for myself, as I can see how hard I am working at being the most whole version of me. My dreams allow me to explore all the contrasts of me as I try out various roles and behaviours—often those I've not been brave enough to attempt in my waking hours.

Depending on what I've been processing in my dreams, sometimes I wake up feeling so much love and peace, and other times, I feel unsettled, as I've obviously been grappling with some deeper-seated emotions. I love the nights when I feel like I'm given a night off to just play; soaring over fields, swimming in tropical paradises or meeting people past and present who I'd love to encounter—or perhaps I'm truly connecting with them in the astral realms.

Anything is possible, and I know there is so much power and wonder within our dreams that we cannot even begin to fathom. Like life, our dream world can be one of paradoxes. It can be a little tumultuous as it heals us, enlightens us, and awakens us to our truth and inner wisdom. It can also be uplifting and inspiring.

I am in awe of the miraculous and mystical nature of our dreams. Your dreams are guided and blessed, just as you are.

Allow your nightly dreams to become a doorway for awakening to and manifesting the dreams you have for your waking life. We can dream our own lives into being. What will you dream?

To manifest our dreams, we need to believe we are powerful enough and worthy enough to receive them. At the same time, we need to combine our intention with action. We can't fail unless we give up, as we are the only ones powerful enough to stop us.

Positive energy and momentum behind our dreams, along with great self-care to make us our most effective, enhances success. Exercising trust and patience while we allow the Universe to catch up with our dreams is key: just because it hasn't happened yet, doesn't mean it won't.

Surrender your dreams and allow the Universe to gift to you all that your heart desires beyond your wildest dreams.

> 'Bless your dreams, your desires and your sense that there is more.
> There is more because you are more.'
> — *Alan Cohen*

It is so important for the manifesting potential of our dreams that we believe that the best is yet to come.
For many of us, life has been a mix of both wonderful and worrisome. Although we've all experienced joy and elation, it is often the tumultuous times that have made their marks on our souls, have challenged us and helped to shape us into the magnificent beings that we have become—that is, after we have cared for and nurtured ourselves and done the deep healing to flourish and bloom.

Hope is the fuel for believing the best is yet to come. We reach for hope every time we embrace optimism and the associated feel-good sensations and thought patterns that coincide with this elevated state.

Reach for life. Don't wait for life to reach you. Act on dreams. Caring for and loving you means that life is waiting for you to have what you most require and desire.

Deep belief in our dreams magnifies our manifesting power.

Energy goes where our attention goes, so pay as little attention as you can to your concerns and as much attention as you can to your dreams.

MESSAGE FOR YOUR PATH TO LOVE

Make dreams a part of your nightly self-care. Dreams provide a clear connection to love while your ego is 'sleeping' and not interfering with your gateways to love through its dramatising or limiting 'viewpoints'. Be free in your sleep and receive a reprieve from day-to-day concerns. Before your slumber, ask for your dream time to help you process issues that you are currently working on and those on a subconscious level that are surfacing to be healed. (Oftentimes, we can shift on a deep level, issues that we are not even fully aware of—and nor do we need to be.)

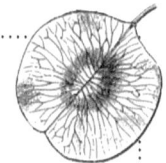

SELF-CARE IDEA FOR TODAY

Establish great conditions for sleep to enhance your ability to dream. Avoid screen time before sleep. Release tension and worry. Address stress levels. Avoid caffeine and alcohol before bed if you want to remember your dreams and be healed by them.

ENERGY CENTRES

Our chakras are energetically spinning balance, power, peace and possibility.

Great self-care is enhanced by learning about and balancing our energy centres. Our chakra energy centres help us to evolve through and activate our greatest potential—accessing all our unique, undiscovered talents and abilities. They contain the codes for our wisdom and wellbeing, allowing both to unfold naturally in a way that is just perfect for us. They hold our life story—past, present and future—and influence every moment of our thoughts, attitudes, beliefs, intentions and actions. They reveal to us what we need to heal, the patterns that no longer serve us and what we need to free for us to truly thrive. Through our energy centres, we become whole and connect fully with the self-care we require to fully embrace our inner wellspring of love.

When our chakras are balanced, we feel alive, confident, powerful and bright within, and able to intuitively make decisions, give and receive love, speak our truth, and use our will to activate meaning and purpose in our lives. When our chakras are clear and balanced, we are our true selves, our best selves—and not the individuals weighed down by the stuff we have taken on from others or by what we have been unable to release within ourselves.

When our chakras are out of balance, we don't feel our best selves. Our stress, anxiety and overwhelm levels increase and we lack energy and motivation. Our boundaries are lacking, and we feel less powerful and less ease within ourselves. We can diminish our connection with others and to the universal wisdom available to us.

Creating a balanced chakra energy system is an essential component of self-care and self-love. Our chakras are key to healthy spiritual, emotional, mental and physical wellbeing. Our chakra energy system underpins and impacts every other system within our body.

If our base chakra, our foundation in life (represented by the colour red) is balanced and clear, we will feel safe, secure, grounded and non-fearful as our natural state. We will feel secure in our ability to provide financially for ourselves and enjoy a sanctuary at home and within our family units. Physically, our base chakra is connected to our adrenal system.

Our second energy centre (associated with the colour orange) is linked to our ability to form intimate connections and meaningful relationships, and to seek pleasure and all that we dream of manifesting. When our sacral chakra is balanced and clear, we will have an openness to new people and new experiences. We trust in our ability to say no and set effective boundaries. We will experience joy and that joy will be a magnet for more joy and what we truly desire and require in life. Our creativity will be in bloom, and we will experience great contentment through our creative projects. On a physical level, this chakra is connected to our reproductive system.

A clear and aligned solar plexus chakra (associated with the colour yellow) will allow us to connect with our own worth, personal identity, confidence and power. We will have a positive self-image. We will have stronger boundaries and act with stronger intent towards bringing our dreams to fruition. Our third chakra is connected to our pancreas.

Having a balanced heart chakra (associated with the colours green and pink) will allow us to connect with love—love for ourselves, for others and for the experiences of our lives. Gratitude and appreciation become an intrinsic part of who we are and how we function. We trust in and are happy with where we are on our journey and where we are heading. We will stay open to love despite what occurs around us. We can forgive ourselves and others. We have effective relationships—balancing both the giving and receiving of love. We can more easily extend kindness, trust, compassion and forgiveness towards others. We will experience greater flow and connection and understanding of our emotions. We allow our heart to lead us, and our mind and heart are more in sync with each other. We will know ourselves intimately, becoming very aware of our needs, and seek to uplift and contribute to the wellbeing of others and the world at large in some way. We will feel connected to the whole of humanity and know that creating love within ourselves influences all that surrounds us. Love within radiates out to others and into the world. Enjoy loving yourself and your life more fully with a clear heart chakra.

When our throat chakra (associated with light blue) is clear and balanced, we express ourselves effectively. It is the centre of communication. We know what to say, when to say it and how to best deliver our message. We can listen to others with presence. We have clear perception. We trust in our inner guidance and are willing and able to express our truth. Physically, our fifth chakra relates to our throat and thyroid.

A clear brow (third-eye) chakra gives us direct access to our intuition, imagination, vision, knowing, perception and foresight. This sixth chakra energy centre is represented by the colour purple. When this chakra is balanced, we feel lighter because we know life presents unlimited possibilities. We connect consistently with our inner guidance and trust it to guide our lives. We connect with our divine purpose, path and mission. Physically, this chakra relates to our pituitary gland and eyes.

A balanced and clear crown chakra allows us to trust in the magnificence, magic, miracles, synchronicities and abundance of the Universe. We know we are connected to the Universe and that it has our back. We perceive ourselves as divine beings always connected to the love and wisdom of the Universe. This glowing white energy centre represents our higher selves and higher thought. It opens us to our spirituality, our higher power. It is the centre of our faith. With a clear, balanced crown chakra, what we yearn for finds us and we manifest much of what is for our highest good into our reality. We no longer do life alone as we have surrendered to something greater, knowing this source is also part of us. We perceive a sense of oneness with all that is and all that is coming. We embrace that we are divine sparks here to express our divinity in our unique way.

To balance and clear our chakras, we can check in with any negative stories we have on repeat about ourselves and others and seek to reframe these into positive beliefs. Awareness opens us to clearing our chakras of any stuck patterns of belief. Gratitude, love and appreciation all help to reconnect us to positive flow and energy. Positive affirmations help to rewire our thinking into a more healing, uplifting system. Familiarise yourself with the work of Louise Hay to fully grasp the power of our thoughts in creating our health and reality. We can swim in oceans or take salt baths to balance our energies. Being in nature helps to restore energetic balance—especially grounding ourselves by walking barefoot on sand or earth.

Connecting with crystals and their amazing properties is great for balancing our chakras. Placing matching crystal colours on the associated chakras helps balance our energies. Many crystals have specific effects on each of the chakras; for example, aquamarine is the crystal of expression and having the courage to express our truth. It is great for fifth-chakra work and for public speakers.

Essential oils are also excellent assistants for clearing and balancing our chakras. For example, frankincense is beneficial for the throat chakra too and assists with clear and effective speaking. There are combination essences available for the specific purpose of clearing our chakras.

Meditation helps to clear our chakra energies as it helps to connect us with our powerful heart-healing capacity. Yoga is also an effective energy clearer: specific poses target different energy centres. Having our energies cleared and balanced through reiki, acupuncture, sound therapy, kinesiology, and other forms of energetic healing is a treat for our entire energetic system.

Our energetic chakra system requires continual upkeep and maintenance, just as our homes and gardens look and feel their best after regular cleaning and clearing. The experience of life—and most importantly, our reactions to it—regularly impacts our chakra health. We become our most powerful, healthy and content selves in a clear energetic state.

Specific crystals to help clear and balance each chakra are:

- Base chakra—red jasper, hematite, obsidian, garnet, black tourmaline
- Sacral chakra—citrine, amber, orange calcite, carnelian
- Solar plexus chakra—yellow apatite, honey calcite, tiger's eye, citrine
- Heart chakra—green tourmaline, rose quartz, emerald, aventurine, prehnite
- Throat chakra—lapis lazuli, aquamarine, amazonite, blue lace agate, blue kyanite
- Third-eye chakra—sodalite, amethyst, purple fluorite, lepidolite
- Crown chakra—clear quartz, Herkimer diamond, selenite, howlite

Matching the colour of the crystal to the colour of each chakra is the easiest way to work with crystals and chakra clearing if you are a beginner.

Some essential oils to assist with balancing and clearing chakras are:

- Base chakra—vetiver, spikenard, patchouli, cypress, cedarwood
- Sacral chakra—sweet orange, ylang-ylang, patchouli, neroli, clary sage
- Solar plexus chakra—sandalwood, lavender, lemongrass, myrrh, black pepper, grapefruit, bergamot
- Heart chakra—rose, pine, jasmine, neroli, geranium, melissa
- Throat chakra—frankincense, blue chamomile, roman chamomile, lavender, peppermint
- Third-eye chakra—lemon, sandalwood, lavender
- Crown chakra—lime, frankincense, helichrysum

MESSAGE FOR YOUR LOVE TO EVOLVE

The sacred energies that course through all living things have been acknowledged throughout history in many cultures. These energies are gaining more and more attention in modern times where the challenges of our time on Earth have meant we are forced to reconnect with ancient, powerful wisdom to heal and thrive on our planet of contrasts.

Care for your chakras to care for you. Balanced chakras open us to the love and potential that is waiting to bloom within us and for us.

SELF-CARE IDEA FOR TODAY

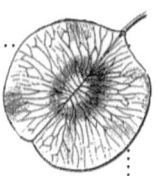

Find a quiet, relaxing place and give yourself a crystal chakra balance. Tune into your crystal collection and see which crystals call to each of your chakras. Program them with the intention of balancing and clearing each chakra. Breathe and connect with your heart space and experience this healing, awakening and healing form of self-care.

EXERCISE

Exercise is the great energy clearer and endorphin creator.

Exercise is perhaps our most natural form of self-care, as our bodies love to move. They let us know in some way or another if we are neglecting our exercise: lethargy, irritation, inflammation, stagnant emotions—it will be different for us all.

Exercise enhances our health. Healthy bodies are more energetic and more vital—leading to greater motivation, peace within and zest for life. The endorphins released during exercise encourage greater positivity within us. Love in the form of elevated emotions often arises through exercise.

Through exercise, we are less judgemental of our appearance. We look good when our bodies are toned and that makes us feel good.

Exercise is as beneficial for the mind as it is for the body. Physically, all systems work better. Exercise makes our bodies and minds feel strong. Mentally, we have greater focus and clarity. Walking is symbolic of moving forward. Every step counts. Exercise grounds us and connects us back into our bodies, back into our hearts and away from mind functioning. The deep breathing clears unwanted energies and emotions. Movement helps to release any build-up of stress or anxiety. Exercise frees us of anything we've taken on from others, as each physical action unlocks anything stuck or stagnant within.

Exercise is moving meditation—when we are focussed on how we are moving and how these movements are feeling, then we are truly present. I love and thrive on the joy of my own presence, and I know you will too as daily concerns disappear into the background. Somehow, things that are troubling us are made less significant through exercise.

Exercise has a magical way of connecting me with my creativity. So often, I will be on my exercise bike, swimming, or out walking when new chapters drop into my mind. I imagine this is because, through exercise, my mind is clear enough to receive the guidance. Exercise releases procrastination and indecision because, as our minds clear, we open more fully to our own intuition and higher guidance—that is, we connect with love. Resistance to what we know we require and desire is released through movement.

Exercise gives me more joie de vivre and more tolerance and compassion for myself and others; enhances gratitude; and promotes less judgement of self and greater connection with my own beauty.

The secret to exercise is finding what you and your body love most. If you don't enjoy your exercise, you will be less motivated to make the necessary commitment required to make it a regular practice. My physical and emotional 'therapy' is swimming. I am so clear, so motivated, so energised, so intoxicated by life after a swim—especially if it is outdoors in nature on a beautiful day.

I don't consider myself to be a true swimmer. My husband calls my type of swimming 'swamming around'. He likens it to a swan just peacefully gliding about. Somehow, it just works for me physically and emotionally, so I will continue to do it no matter what it looks like.

MESSAGE FOR YOUR PATH TO LOVE

Exercise magically reminds me of the love that already exists for my body, for me and for my life. It has the power to heal and transform on levels beyond our human understanding. It makes us feel good. We feel more alive and more inspired—and that is love in action.
Exercise develops discipline: great self-care practices require commitment to make the changes in attitude and lifestyle for love to flourish.

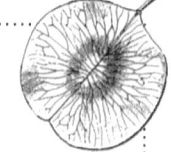

SELF-CARE IDEA FOR TODAY

The ability to move is a gift. Make the choice to move.
How will you move your body today?
Try something new each day until you find something that lights you up and makes your body feel great.

FANTASY

Fantasy is our reminder of the magic that exists within us and all around us.

Fantasy is a great healer as it assists us to escape reality when a reprieve—a mind-clearing reset—is most needed. It provides a beautiful distraction from what life may be currently presenting. The joy associated with fantasy elevates us to a new space of being and opens us to new realities and new possibilities.

Fantasy is healing because it releases stress and therefore enhances our immune system. Fantasy can also ignite our imagination and enhance creativity and inspiration. It returns us to the halcyon days of our childhood where fantasy and magic prevailed. It connects us with childlike wonder and contentment and carries us into the space of remembering and believing that the extraordinary may just be possible.

I love unicorns. Each time I see an image of one of these mystical, magical, beautiful beings, I feel uplifted. I imagine you have your own magical equivalent that you could reconnect with. Unicorns invoke feelings of childlike innocence, purity and wonder. They remind me of the love within me and the love that abounds in life. They signify the possibilities for miracles and magic to unfold in my life at any moment. Miracles are a true companion of love. I am ready for miracles and so are you.

A beautiful part of fantasy is that it connects us with and reminds us of magic and of our own ability to create it. As young children, we were often given magic wands as part of our play. What if we could reinstate our belief in making wishes and having them fulfilled? Wishes are a beautiful form of self-care and a gift to our soul. Wishes elevate our emotions and they remind us to connect with something so powerful and miraculous that anything is possible. Wishes invoke magic and a sense of mystical possibility. When we make a wish, we are still, present and powerful.

When was the last time you made a wish?

- Wish upon a star.
- Catch the tails of a shooting star; allow it to take you places you never dreamed of previously.
- Step into the unknown and make a wish from there—and surrender to the miracles waiting to unfold just for you.
- Make a wish when you see a rainbow—the ultimate sign of hope and blessings to come.
- Make a wish when you see a feather—just maybe, the angels will take your wish straight to Heaven. Wish fulfilled.
- Wish on the power of repeating numbers: 11.11, 1.11 and 333 are my favourites.
- Blow the seeds from a dandelion and make a wish.
- Light a candle and make a wish.
- Look at images of unicorns and magical beings and make a wish.
- Catch a fairy (thistledown) and make a wish.
- Make a wish for each of the birthday candles you blow out.
- Make a wish when you cut your wedding (or any celebration) cake.

What will you wish for today?

- I wish to quickly release the experience of the pain of others and transmute it into love.
- I wish that [name of person] heals quickly and with ease.
- I wish [name of person] finds peace, love and their own power and potential.
- I wish for my work or creative output to enrich the lives of others.
- I wish for abundance and love in all its many forms to flood my world.
- I wish for great adventures and opportunities around every corner.
- I wish for that which lights me up to make its way to me every day.
- I wish for all beings to remember that they are free and that it is a free-will universe.
- I wish for peace within, in life, and for the world.
- I wish to be empowered and revitalised by optimal health.

MESSAGE FOR YOUR PATH TO LOVE

Be and feel your most fantastic by connecting with fantasy. Fill your life with sparks of joy and possibility. Rise above the mundane into the extraordinary. If you need reminders, tap into the movie or reading worlds of fantasy.

SELF-CARE IDEA FOR TODAY

Our wishes are powerful prayers that travel out into the Universe. Connect your wishes with love and they will be mega magical wishes. Wishes are powerful for ourselves and others when they are infused with love. Place your hand on your heart (our portal for love) and wish away.

FASHION

Beautiful clothes are gifts to our senses, hearts and bodies.

Putting effort into selecting your outfit each day is putting effort into you, caring for you and loving you. It is a creative, meditative experience. It may not be something you feel inspired to do every day, but when it does 'call', it's very uplifting. Feeling your absolute best is what you deserve and will certainly get your day off to a beautiful, high-vibe start.

Wearing gorgeous clothes can make us feel special and beautiful. It can connect us with our joy, love, creativity, inspiration and aliveness.

Fashion can take our focus away from a phenomenon I have termed 'face stress'. Many women, including young women, struggle to see the beauty in their faces as society tells them that facial lines are the enemy. Face stress is a result of years of exposure and unfavourable comparison to images of otherworldly perfection in airbrushed magazines and via the proliferation of enhanced, fully tweaked and perfectly polished social media images. These images remove all signs of beautiful facial expressions, as they have been deemed undesirable. This unnatural state is a costly one—costing time, resources, money and self-worth—as there is always something that needs improving. It trains individuals to look at what is 'wrong' rather than what is very right and very beautiful. We do not need to be cloned to fit one standard of beauty. Just as we have diversity in our fashion sense, we can have diversity in our physical appearance.

Focus on the beauty of the dress you're wearing, the fabric, the way it moves in the breeze, the intricate details, how it was cut to flatter and accentuate all that you love about you. Beautiful dresses are a celebration of life. Wear them whenever and wherever the mood strikes and not just for special occasions. Every day we are alive is a celebration. We are the chosen ones as we are on planet Earth.

I perceive that part of the reason I love dresses is that they remind me of carefree, balmy summer days. When wearing dresses, I have a definite holiday feeling, probably because during my teaching days I was on holidays for a large part of summer. Tasmanian summers are quite fleeting some years, so I am a dress opportunist—basking in the floaty, elegant feeling of wearing a dress whenever I can.

Dresses are my friends. I have many in my wardrobe that are over twenty years old, and they still come out to shine every now and then. Many of these vintage pieces contain gorgeous memories of places and experiences I've had whilst wearing them.

All forms of fashion light us up as it is a beautiful form of creative expression. I went through a stage of remodelling a lot of older clothing, which also allowed me to express my creativity without over-consuming. Some days, I love my jeans or athletic wear, and on other days, it will be dresses—contrasts light me up with clothing as variety is the spice of life and all that! One friend even commented that fashion was her favourite sport! As I don't play sport, it is now definitely my favourite sport also.

Each day, we can tune into what our bodies and souls would like to wear, and honour that—a beautiful form of self-care. Listening to our bodies and hearts and putting something on that feels great can make such a difference to our days.

I remember one year, I had a particularly demanding class, and each day was like going into battle with the hope that I would survive. My husband would often text and say, *How is your day going?* My reply was often, *All good because I have my favourite boots on*, etc. My clothing drew my focus away from perceived duress and towards beauty within and around me. Whatever works! Clothes light me up every day.

I experienced the power of dresses and the vibrations of love that they can bring on a recent holiday. There is a place on the island where people gather to celebrate the beauty of the sun going down. It is always a high-vibrational experience as people connect with the most resplendent display of nature and the power of her beauty. While I was absorbed in the spectacle before me, a gorgeous little girl came towards me to say hello. She had a pretty dress on that I could tell was lighting her up—she was connecting with the power of dresses from an early age. I spoke to her and told her that her dress was beautiful. Well, she beamed! I think she grew two centimetres and her energy radiated outwards instantly. I was reminded of the extreme power of compliments for both the giver and receiver. She loved this so much, and being the generous little soul that she was, she obviously wanted to share this experience. Less than two minutes later, she returned with a little friend who was also wearing a lovely dress. She straight away asked me if I liked her friend's dress. Once again, I showered another little girl in heartfelt comments about the beauty of her dress and she had a similar and equally wonderful reaction. It was such a simple and beautiful experience of love.

To this day, when I recall these moments, they bring tears of joy to my eyes, and I know those little girls, wherever they are in the world, benefitted from meeting me and the energy of love and beauty that we shared.

Next time you see someone wearing something you admire, let them know and you will flood them with the energy of love.

MESSAGE FOR YOUR LOVE TO BLOOM

One day, I called into a supermarket on my way out to lunch—the attendant loved my dress and asked if I was off to a special occasion. I thought to myself, *Yes, I'm alive and healthy, so every day is a special occasion.*

Any of us who have had health issues know that wellness after long-term health battles is sublime and every day is indeed cause for celebration. Wear that special dress today!

Don't ever underestimate the power of a dress or your fashion equivalent to invoke love—love of beauty and love of the self within the dress!

SELF-CARE IDEA FOR TODAY

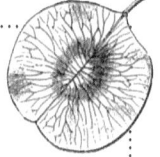

Wear a favourite outfit today no matter what the occasion, just because you are worth it. Most importantly, as part of your self-care and self-love protocols, be willing to receive compliments graciously. Compliments are a gift to the receiver and the giver.

FEATHERED FRIENDS

*Birds remind us to soar above
our limitations and choose freedom.*

Birds are a work of art and a tribute to the miraculous wonder of nature. They are an engineering marvel inspiring mankind to dream big and to create in an unlimited manner. Birds inspired us to take to the sky and still encourage us to soar.

There's a lot to be learned from birds. Our feathered companions remind us that we are free, even at times when our minds convince us otherwise. We can always rise above our current situation and take a bird's eye view, a new perspective.

I regularly watch through my window and see all different species of birds happily coexisting side by side, just doing their own unique thing, sharing the food provided by Mother Earth. Imagine if all the different races, religions and beings on planet Earth could share resources and inhabit the same space peacefully.

Our feathered friends provide us with self-care opportunities simply through their presence, beauty and energy. Birds connect us with wonder and awe and our ability to see the extraordinary around us, waiting to be witnessed by and appreciated by us. Gratitude is an essential part of self-care: that is, tapping into elevated emotions just through the way we respond to, connect with, and appreciate all of life. Birds provide many opportunities for feelings of gratitude. Their mere existence is a blessing to us if we choose to connect with their vibration and witness them.

Birds leave us gifts that fall in front of our path: their feathers. Many believe that white feathers are gifts from angels, a sign that they are with us. Feathers always seem to lift our spirits. Many people like to have them in their homes for their positive energy. Feathers connote an element of air-clearing energy.

Birds are messengers from spirit. They serve as a connection from our earthly world to the heavenly realms. Birds soar above earthly matters and resonate with enlightenment and peace. They sing for us every morning, heralding in a new day of unlimited possibilities.

Upon awaking, rather than tuning into my own thoughts, I often tune into the sounds and chatter of the birds. This helps me to break free of any conditioned thought patterns that flood in while on autopilot. I feel the vibration of the birds, their energy, their states of love *before* I allow my own thoughts to glide in. This helps me to manifest positive, high-vibrational thinking rather than unconsciously reach for a to-do list or an inventory of worry.

Birdsong calls us to states of love. Birds remind us of the qualities of gentleness, softness, elegance and freedom; they can fly whenever and wherever they choose.

Different angels and archangels resonate with certain birds and animals. I perceive a connection with Archangel Raphael through green birds. Often, after client sessions, green rosellas would be fossicking on the lawn outside my rooms and I would hear, *I am with you. Together we will bring healing to the world, one person at a time.* This was such a beautiful acknowledgement of the teaching, healing and transformation I was encouraging for my clients. I felt so very loved and extremely grateful that I was able to do the uplifting work that I enjoy.

Before my book launch, I had a magical experience with another green bird. The launch was a large occasion for me. It was the first time I had been truly visible with my work in front of an audience. A beautiful bird with iridescent green wings and zebra stripes hit my window and dropped on its back in front of me. The words infused through my mind were, *Here I am. I am here. I am here.* Once again, I felt the presence and support of

Archangel Raphael with the words *It's time to take flight* flowing through me. I reikied this gorgeous little bird and stroked him and cuddled him. He sat on my finger for some time, and I relished the loving energy. When he was ready, he took flight, which is, metaphorically speaking, what I needed to do on book launch day! It was quite the analogy for me, and during the book launch, the energy of love was high; I felt the presence of angels throughout all proceedings, including my speech. I felt truly blessed and knew that my book had a greater purpose.

At a resort retreat that I visited, I tuned into bird chatter, and for whatever reason I heard, *You're so pretty, you're so pretty*. Maybe spirit was reminding me to be especially kind to myself that day—and that one can choose to feel pretty on any given day, at any age, in any situation.

I'm not entirely sure how these messages from spirit occur via birds, but really listen and tune in and you may be very surprised and delighted at what flows into your mind. Birds always take me straight to elevated emotions through the wonder and awe that is inspired within me. I feel aligned and connected with my higher self in the magical presence of birds.

Each bird that I observe or connect with brings with it different symbolism. Connect with your own version of this symbolism for it to reveal intuitive messages for you and serve as a foray into the mystical elements of life.

There are also some universal associations that can add to our repertoire for understanding bird symbolism. For example, doves are often a symbol of peace and harmony, and owls imply wisdom.

Here are some feathered friends that particularly resonate with me:

- Owls—I would often see images of owls when I was creating *Pearls of Wisdom: For Your Path to Peace*. For me, it was an acknowledgement of being on the right track.

- Green birds—reminders to seek and receive abundance in its many forms: love, beauty, healing, great connections and wealth.
- Swans—signify grace, elegance and beauty.
- Peacocks—show up, shine and be your own star.
- Ravens—a reminder to look deeper and to embrace the mystical, magical realms.
- Kookaburras—laugh more, don't make anything significant and prepare for the earth to be washed clean; rain is on the way.
- Blue cranes—my blue cranes have lived with us for decades and often sit on our roof. They are symbols of peace, blessings and good luck. They seem to look at me with a deep knowing, soothing my soul with a reminder of the power of quiet elegance and deep wisdom.
- Eagles—eagles flying over our farm remind me of stepping into our power, seeing from a higher perspective, soaring to new heights, and rising above earthly concerns to gain fresh insight.
- Blue wrens—quiet, unassuming beauty.
- Swallows—be industrious and avoid underestimating the power of the 'tiny' or the true magnitude of small steps.
- Sulphur-crested cockatoos—these gorgeous little creatures invoke pure joy for me. They light up my heart and take me straight to love. They are so trusting and will stay and 'chat' for lengthy periods of time, making me very present, still and calm. They are great listeners. They remind me to embrace playfulness, mischief and adaptability. I gleefully watched their ingenuity when on an island vacation. One character flew down, nabbed a little butter container, gently prized it open with his beak and eagerly devoured the contents. I was enthralled.
- Doves—remind me to seek to harmonise situations and

allow peace to flow within.
- Hummingbirds—a reminder of how the tiniest actions can often yield the mightiest results.
- Ducks—show me the power of gentle, unhurried presence.

MESSAGE FOR YOUR LOVE TO BLOOM

Listen to birdsong. Tune your vibration to the high vibration of birds. Clear your mind, activate total presence—and see what messages they have for you. Ask to attune to the vibration of their love and feel the uplifting within your heart.

Become aware of birds that repeatedly cross your path, either physically or via images. Research their symbolism and connect with your own inner wisdom to ascertain what messages may be occurring for you.

Slow down, observe, and connect with the wonder and awe of the bird kingdom: self-care in action.

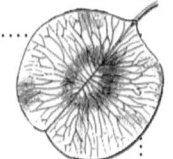

SELF-CARE IDEA FOR TODAY

Learning to rise above our daily concerns and find our own version of beautiful freedom-inducing wings is self-care. Write down the three things that are most concerning you at this current time. Burn the piece of paper and at the same time say three times, 'I let this all fly away from me. It is free; I am free.' Rituals are a nurturing form of self-care.

FEELING FREE

The seeds of our freedom are grown in the mind. Water yours often.

Circumstances external to us often appear to take our freedom. But do they really? Or do we hijack our own freedom through our responses to experiences we feel we can't control?

There are many situations we find ourselves in that will challenge our sense of freedom. It may be lockdown, carer roles, parenting and step-parenting demands, responsibilities at work, thwarted travel opportunities, or unfounded fear in taking a new direction. The list is endless.

Freedom is created in the mind, and often what we resist persists. Our minds have this uncanny way of telling us that we need to be someplace other than where we are currently at—indicating that where we are isn't quite good enough and perhaps not where we can be most happy. There is a tendency to want to escape our current reality rather than face it head-on, appreciate what is right about it and change what needs to really change—which is how we feel and function in said circumstances. The 'escape' comes first from within and is more about attitude than location. If we don't address what is causing the unrest or unease within, we will take this state or stance with us wherever we go.

What if you could be happy with wherever you are and with whatever you are doing? When you've achieved this, you are at your most powerful and the world is yours to create as you dream it. As I say in *Pearls of Wisdom: For Your Path to Peace*, 'the world is your oyster, and it can create many pearls.'

We can handle so much more than we ever give ourselves

credit for. We are not given anything we can't handle in life. Much of what occurs for us contains opportunities for our growth. We need to develop freedom around our reactions. Being kind to ourselves by removing judgement around how we feel and how we react creates freedom. This, combined with choices that allow us to feel more expansive and freer, is great self-care. Dropping resistance to what is and instead embracing gratitude for what is, is key. Release expectations around situations, experiences and people.

In all of life, there is always a silver lining: an opportunity for growth, wisdom and potential to emerge. Pressure creates diamonds!

The world climate and life in general are highly challenging and testing us all on many levels—both acknowledged and unacknowledged. Many of us have experienced a sense of wanting to 'escape'. The thing is, there is no escape from our reality, only the chance to create a new one. We do this (as you will be aware after reading *Pearls*) by looking within and seeing what our current reality is trying to reveal to us. Our reality is created for us and by us. It is designed to test us so that we expand and grow and release anything that is holding us back from creating a reality that is aligned with how we want to feel, be, and experience our life.

You don't need to escape your current life; just care for yourself and love yourself enough to take the steps required to create a better one. We can't buy or drink our way out of our reality; we can't move jobs or town or country to avoid it. It will follow us. Your circumstances are created by you and for you. Yes, world events and other influences outside of our control can have an impact, but we still create our own reality within the larger reality through our beliefs, energy, attitudes and choices.

We expand and grow most when we are challenged. How are you currently testing yourself? How is life testing you? What is it trying to show you? Get the wisdom behind it all and you can change it and create something more in alignment with how you want to feel, be, and experience life. Face it all to change it all. You can because you're way more powerful than you realise. Right where you are, there are possibilities for peace, happiness and new directions.

Feel where you are at without resistance. Be open to lots of seeing and learning how and why you've created what you've created. Start with where you're at today. Change your attitude, make small but pivotal changes, believe in greater possibilities. If we keep being the same, life continues to reproduce the same—you're that powerful.

What is showing up in your life right now is trying to show you something. Perhaps it is that you are worth more and deserve more and need to choose more. Perhaps there are things you are refusing to let go of that are keeping you stuck in an all-too-familiar cycle.

Change in your outside world originates from within. Do the work to set yourself free, to create, and dream, and expand, and create some more. A big life is calling to you. Can you hear its gentle whispers …?

MESSAGE FOR YOUR PATH TO LOVE

Grant yourself the gift of freedom this day by stepping into a place of allowance. Be thankful for everything that is occurring, with no complaints. Be for life, not against it. We need to be able to embrace all of life, including the challenges. Our self-care and love help us to access this place of allowing within, as we learn to flow with life rather than resist it.

SELF-CARE IDEA FOR TODAY

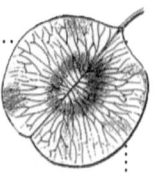

We always have a choice in how we perceive and respond to a situation. How will you take care of you through your reactions today? Choose responses that assist you to feel a greater sense of freedom.

FIREWORKS

Allow your self-care to fire and light you up.

I recently experienced spectacularly amazing fireworks to the point that it felt like I'd never seen pyrotechnics before. I was totally captivated and absorbed in firecracker beauty. My husband and I (along with approximately two hundred others) were standing in the pouring rain under large umbrellas after a gala dinner that in itself was magical, and the fireworks hadn't even begun.

The anticipation for what was to come was just beautiful for me. The fireworks began in an explosion of colour and accompanying music. A feast for the senses. My husband was just as captivated by my facial expressions as he was by the fireworks. Apparently, I appeared mesmerised (I most certainly was) and my level of awe, wonder and childlike joy had him as equally entranced as the fireworks did.

My experience of these fireworks was different to any other. It was like I was surrounded by stars, had become the stars, was immersed by stunning jewels and the magic of enchanted worlds all in one. Each mini explosion filled me with intense light, love and power. It reminded me of how **love elevates us to receive the extraordinary.**

I was totally and completely present; I felt the joy of my own presence and that of all of life. These splendiferous fireworks contained beauty second after second, reinventing itself in a myriad of new ways moment to moment.

The experience showed me the power of surrendering to the beautiful unknown and responding beyond our senses—that is, from the universal love.

MESSAGE FOR YOUR LOVE TO BLOOM

There is something out there that fills you with awe and wonder. It may not be something that traditionally inspires these feelings—but it does for you. Find it and witness it. There is no better form of self-care or access to the love within than responding with awe to what is all around you.

Get to know yourself. Only you know what truly lights you up and fires that special something within.

SELF-CARE IDEA FOR TODAY

Find something, perhaps in nature, or as part of what you already enjoy doing, and be so present within the moment and so connected to the love within you that it becomes an elevated energy experience. Focus on gratitude, awe and wonder, and keep building these qualities within the moment. You will move beyond the ordinary to the extraordinary just through the power of you and your responses. This is beautiful self-care and access to love.

FLOWERS

Flowers are analogies in action, teaching us to live harmoniously with all of life.

Flowers symbolise love and beauty and remind us to connect with this essence within ourselves and in others: our true nature. They are unique, special and diverse, as are all creatures and beings on Earth. Flowers are gifts from Mother Nature to light us up and nourish our hearts. Flowers teach us to connect with the cycles and seasons: sometimes we can be in bloom and at other times we are just watering and nourishing our seeds. Sometimes, we like to be on show and highly visible, and at other times, we may like to be retreating into the background.

A vital part of our self-care is knowing when to expand our energy and when to conserve it. We can't always be in radiant bloom. We need to be at peace and accepting of all our many seasons and cycles, trusting in the miraculous nature of life.

'If flowers know exactly when and how to bloom, then you do too.'
— Rebecca Campbell

Flowers signify peace because they just 'be'. They weather all storms and bloom when the time is right. They flow with life and surrender to what is occurring. They don't hold on to their blooms; they allow their petals to be what they are, when they are.

Different flowers speak to us in a variety of ways. As we are all diversely different, so too will our responses be to various flowers. Find those you are most drawn to; those that open your heart with their beauty, symbolic meaning and energy. They can be great teachers. Flowers help us to be present enough to connect with our higher selves when we are captivated by their beauty and aroma.

These are some of my responses to favourite flowers and the symbolism and meaning they invoke within me:

Camellias

One day, while I was observing camellias unfold on my tree, there was a single lone bloomer. It reminded me that someone always needs to be willing to go first, to lead … and sometimes that needs to be me.

Peonies

These little beauties are miracles in action. They appear as very understated and non-attention-drawing, and then unfold into something beyond spectacular. They teach us to patiently wait for the magic. They remind us to connect with that sense within that knows there's something bursting to reveal itself.

Dahlias

Dahlias have hundreds of tiny parts forming one spectacular whole, as do we.

Daphne

The smell of daphne is divinely intoxicating and reaches far in a home to elevate the energy with the presence of its perfume and beauty.

Roses

Allow your beauty to unfold and show itself to the world. With enough light, we open, we bloom. Roses are often associated with love that arises from deep within the heart. Wisdom also blossoms from within the heart: the wisdom that arises after we've processed life, and most importantly, our reactions to it. A rose has many beautiful layers that reveal themselves one petal at a time. We can do the same.

Tulips

Tulips remind us that light and beauty await underneath the darkness.

Pink tulips remind me to be and receive love and to know that it can unfold anywhere. I love the delicate cups holding surprise-filled centres. They are perfection unveiling themselves for others to enjoy.

I love the contrast of the slender stems emerging from succulent leaves. We are beings of contrast and need to relish in this.

Dogwoods

Dogwoods signify the many changing faces of beauty. Their blooms start as white, then merge to yellow and next transform to pink. Next, there is the creation of a berry. Their blooms bear fruit. When we bloom, we can also bear great fruit!

In winter, they take a deep, long rest, ready for huge flourishing and radiating in the summer months. Sometimes, large restoration periods are required for us too!

Flowering cherries

Flowering cherries remind me to embrace all the seasons as the blooms show up and shine only seasonally and very briefly, which is better than not at all. Pink and white flowers always invoke feelings of love and peace for me.

Hydrangeas

The deep, rich, powerful colours of hydrangeas, combined with the beautiful shade variants contained within each flower, make up glorious unfolding balls of beauty. There is such diversity, just as there is within us.

Asiatic lilies

Asiatic lilies teach us about being willing to let go when it's time to let go. Holding on too tightly, for too long, and asking for more than is being offered can create a mess—as anyone who has kept a bunch of lilies in a vase for too long can attest. As the petals drop, so too do the stamens—creating quite a clean-up as stamen dust stains where it lands. These lilies enjoy a long blooming season; once they release their beauty into the world, they are not afraid to shine at length for the duration.

MESSAGE FOR YOUR LOVE TO SEED AND FLOURISH

Flowers are rich in their diversity and beauty, as are you. They thrive and bloom with much nourishment, water and sunshine. They gift us love via their beauty. Receive their ever-present love and the corresponding love within you by bringing flowers into your world. If you can't access fresh flowers, source some dried arrangements, or hang pictures of flowers on your walls.

SELF-CARE IDEA FOR TODAY

Pick a beautiful flower, hold it to your heart and receive its beauty and yours. Place it in a vase so you can connect with its essence throughout the day.

I recently visited a tulip farm and was immediately transported to my kind of heaven. As I watched the hearts of the tulips opening to the sun, I felt an opening of my own heart.

Find a flower farm near you and immerse yourself in radiant, nourishing beauty.

HERO'S JOURNEY

*Be your own hero;
they desperately seek you.*

Many of us undertake our very own hero journey: a path that requires so much of our courage, our bravery, our light, our hope, our resources, and our unwavering trust and relentless unstoppability. These journeys can feel more like missions as they require so much of our mental, emotional, physical and spiritual reserves. Nothing is guaranteed or assured on these journeys, yet we plough ahead anyway with nothing but uncertain outcomes and what feels like a divine calling as our driving force. There is no guaranteed prize at the end of the journey—whether that be in terms of success, accolades, encouragement, or financial reward.

These missions, callings or journeys are successful only through extreme self-care and connection with our deepest reserves of love. This is because the nature of these uniquely travelled paths requires so much of us. We step into the unknown daily and must face our own wounds, limitations and trauma along the way.

To be a hero for others, we have to get free of anything that stands in the way of our own potential, light and love, as that makes us most effective in our service.

I believe we all have our own version of a hero's journey (or several) throughout our lifetime. Some journeys require several strength-building missions in the lead-up to develop the necessary power, resilience, faith, skills, knowledge and fortitude required for the next leg of the journey.

My early hero journeys involved divorce, loss and losing my eyesight through a failed routine laser surgery procedure to correct mild short-sightedness. This phase was the most harrowing and tested me beyond what I initially thought I was capable of enduring. Suffice to say, it took me along a new path complete with my newly acquired sixth sense and the emergence of new talents and abilities that would ultimately prepare me for my greatest hero journey: becoming a writer and author.

Becoming a writer and author helped to uncover all that was within me calling to show up for me and others. It provided daily entry into completely unknown territory and required deep healing; connecting to my inner guidance; becoming free of my unwillingness to be seen and heard; learning to speak my truth to heal myself and others (without the fear of judgement or rejection holding me back) and connecting with and trusting my muses, who would often show up at around 3.30 am to 4.00 am, as that was when I was most clear and receptive and least resistant.

All hero journeys require great personal transformation to be carried out successfully. My writing involved much learning from life, as I was given opportunities to experience all that wanted to be written through me, for the world. There were many highs and lows and great quests and personal challenges that arose before coming out the other side with beautiful words flowing onto pages. There were also limiting beliefs and doubts that had to be overcome and that can be most easily captured with the niggling point of view, *Who am I to write a book and however will I get it out into the world?* I had to unlearn some limiting behaviours that were in the way of my mission.

With writing (and I imagine it is the same with your hero journey) there are no guarantees; we cannot be vested in any outcomes. The publishing journey is a difficult one for most to navigate. There are proposals to write that may never see the light of day; questions around which publishing house to select; extreme costs, if you are self-publishing; lack of communication from publishers who have their own set of important tasks to perform; and not having a profile or platform to launch yourself and your work into the world.

All heroes in all fields need faith that something larger than us is at play, and that our work is very much needed in the world and, in some way and somehow, will find its way to those who most need it. Trusting in our own guidance and intuition is paramount in knowing when and how to act.

Find anchors that will support you on your hero journey and hold on to them tightly. These anchors, for me, have been:

- Self-care that changes as I change and can vary day to day according to what I most desire and require for moving forward and connecting with love.
- Trusting that I don't need to know 'how' to get my books into the world, as it will reveal itself at the right time and in the right way for my highest good and for those I will serve through this work.
- Extreme faith in my muses and the process and creativity that we are embarking on together.
- Belief in myself and my work even on days when it momentarily slides.
- Compassion for myself and the totality of the experience, including all the highs and lows.
- The acknowledgement and honouring of the personal healing required along the way.
- Being unstoppable in the face of challenges and adversity.
- Holding on to the words of Reid Tracy when he told us at a Hay House Writer's Conference that even if only one person reads our work and is changed by it, then it is worth it.
- My readers: their beautiful feedback on my first book,

Pearls of Wisdom: For Your Path to Peace, has been a great source of fuel for me to keep going with this book and commit to helping it find its way into the world for them and new readers.

- My husband's unwavering belief in me has been my shooting star to hold on to throughout my hero's journey. Who or what can be your shooting star?

MESSAGE FOR YOUR PATH TO LOVE

Believe in yourself wholeheartedly. Stay in your lane. Let the doubts and opinions of others become white noise. You are guided and on track. Success is imminent. Connect with love; support yourself with extreme self-care and do the work that is calling to you.

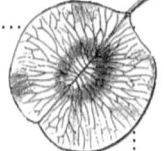

SELF-CARE IDEA FOR TODAY

Read or connect with others who have undergone their own hero's journey for inspiration and motivation.

IF NOT NOW, WHEN?

Change creates new spaces and places just for you.

Change is inevitable. Nothing ever stays the same, so we may as well embrace the truth that we grow and evolve most as our inner and outer worlds change. It is largely up to us if we want small change or grand change. Keep in mind that the more monumental changes often lead to a larger, more expansive life. If we keep being and doing the same, we get more of the same.

Change occurs most often in association with two contrasting states.

One form of change being accessed is via the experience of rock-bottom times, when we are forced to change to survive or thrive.

Change often occurs after upheaval. Sometimes, we can't see what needs to change unless we receive a shake-up, wake-up of some kind. Just think of the destruction that is evident during home renovations before the beautiful new creations are revealed. Our footings often need a nudge before we will let go of control and any limiting status quo.

Many of us hold on to things for too long out of fear of loss—that part of us that does not want to let go of the old to make space for newer versions of us.

We are currently renovating, and as a nature lover, my heart hurt when we were not able to save a couple of trees in the process. I had to let go of what was and embrace a bigger picture, even though all I could see was destruction. I trusted that, out of the rubble, something spectacular would emerge.

The other common change-invoking state is peace. When we feel safe and calm, we are better equipped to cope with the demands of looking within to reveal our current limitations or long-held trauma. We are also less resistant to change during peaceful times.

Our self-care is vital for each paradoxical version of change, first to allow us to access the necessary calm to soothe enough to open to release and change, and second to give us the strength to cope with the change being demanded of us through extreme adversity and duress. Both scenarios will require very different forms of self-care. Connecting with our inner guidance and love assists us to determine what we require for the change that is calling for us. Expertly matching our self-care with our needs is key to successfully manifesting the desired and required change.

A client recently asked, 'How do I let go of things that are preventing change, that I can't seem to release?' Firstly, we acknowledged that having this awareness was a great step in the right direction. Secondly, we worked on finding the truth within the situation she could not release and discovered that she did not trust people and struggled to form friendships because of bullying in her teen years. Next, we looked at the bigger picture—what was the lesson in the bullying? We determined that she had not ever been willing to speak her truth, claim her power or access her self-worth. Her boundaries were weak, making her a perfect target for bullies who love to drain the energy of others as they are not good at generating their own.

Awareness creates the ability to change. Cultivating our inner worth grows our self-love. From here, we develop the power to let go, to forgive, and to change anything that is in the way of our peace and contentment.

Moving forward, my client could now forgive, let go, and appreciate what the bullying experience had shown her. Perhaps it had even been a gift for her evolution? Sometimes, the meanest characters on our life stage give us the unpleasant 'encouragement' we require to step up, change, and claim more of ourselves and our power. My client was willing to change all that was in the way of developing trust in friendships. Using self-care to develop greater self-love, self-worth, and the ability to access and speak her truth became her focus for the coming months. She was able to transform fear into power.

Change brings to us what is more in alignment with who we are becoming and how we want to feel and function in life. These changes are what we have asked for, or yearned for, even if only on a subconscious level. Resisting these changes is resisting you and all you can have and be. Choose surrender and flow and each rite of passage leading to change will be less tumultuous for you.

Surrendering to life on life's terms with awareness and intuitive action is the perfect panacea for change. Resisting change is resisting the beautiful unfolding of you and your potential. Resist nothing, BE everything. Welcome your personal transformation and greatness with an open heart and loving arms. You and your life are worth it.

MESSAGE FOR YOUR LOVE TO BLOOM

Change and her big sister, transformation, occur through
our self-care and connection to love. These facets create
the foundation of peace and trust necessary for creating the
possibility of portals of change opening within us and for us.
Change stirs our potential, providing the seeds for our greatness
to bloom. Allow the loving, gentle whispers of your soul to be
heard through your self-care during those times when your
guard is down enough to receive some new awareness. If not
now, when?

SELF-CARE IDEA FOR TODAY

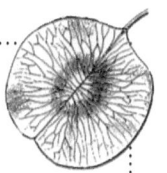

Change in our outer landscape arises from change in our inner landscape. Review any personal limiting stories that may be keeping your change at bay. Have your journal ready and ask, *What is the truth here that I have been unwilling or unable to see?* Great change means releasing all that is unfulfilling to make way for what can be extremely gratifying. Unearth you by finding the treasure held within change.

INNER PEACE

*Change your level of peace,
change your level of life.*

Even though I have written a whole book about finding our peace, my understanding and connection with it is ever-evolving. The experience of peace and its associated calm and contentment is like finding a pot of gold at the end of every rainbow and all its equivalents.

On my husband's recent birthday, I asked him what he wished for most in the upcoming year. His response was 'peace and abundance.' This actually surprised me, as he runs several businesses and is always creating, expanding, successful, not easily ruffled, and on top of things. I had underestimated his desire for these states and at the same time I was reminded of why he is as effective in life as he is: he values peace and contentment and knows that he attracts more (and with greater ease and flow) from this powerful space. He has come to appreciate that power in the business world (and in all elements of life) is most effective when it is more gentle than forceful and arises more fully through our peace. I felt the depth of his understanding of the power and purpose of peace in our lives: the knowing that all that is great and good and abundant in our lives flourishes through a calm nervous system and inner space.

We all experience moments of deep peace and the accompanying break from the incessant mind chatter and accompanying emotions. Take yourself to your place of peace through whatever means required to remind yourself of how it feels.

For many, peace is only there for extended periods when on holiday: think tropical paradise, sun streaming on our bodies, blue sky, crashing white waves, and nowhere to be and nothing to do other than what calls to us in each precious moment. The reality is that for most of us, stepping into our day-to-day existence can make inner peace quite elusive. To be peace, we must first uncover all that we have placed in the way of it, and unlearn much of what society has told us is real, true and important. Uncovering our own unique truth and wisdom is key.

My first book takes us on a journey through many scenarios and life themes where we can unlock our peace through listening to the wisdom of our own soul—our personal inner guide through life. I would recommend making *Pearls* your companion for a time as a beautiful self-care seed. It will teach you how to care for yourself enough, to commit to yourself enough, to turn all that life throws at you—all the adversity, all the challenges—into a platform from which you can access your peace and launch it into your life and into the world.

Our peace needs to be our primary daily purpose, not something we attempt to find for five minutes when all else and sundry is done. We need to tune into it with great commitment. If you are anything like me, it is an ever-changing landscape. If we are not peaceful, our inner wisdom is calling us to make some changes on a physical, mental, emotional or spiritual level. It may be as simple as an attitude adjustment, changing our current line of thought, eating something that makes our body feel good, meditation, or time in nature for a reset. We need to access our self-care toolkit most frequently. We also need to have compassion for ourselves and patience during the times and days when we don't feel good. Life is contrasts; it's not always in rosy bloom. We need an optimistic stance of 'this too shall pass' as part of our personal self-care package.

For us to create the life that Universe most desires for us—

one where our dreams are fulfilled and we feel amazing during the unfoldment—we need to make peace and calm our natural default system. Out of our peace arises our greatest potential for love. Free your peace; it is your divine birthright. Face all that stands in its way by bringing your best self-care to heal the fear that is calling to be released.

Let go, let go, forever let go and let love and peace reign.

Develop a deep reverence for your life. Understand that it is all for you. All the experiences are woven into the tapestry of your life for the greatest unfolding of you and your glory and potential. Embrace it all, as what could be more perfect for you?

A possible entry point for finding your peace may be by going back in time to your childhood. Connect with your inner child at a time when they were most at peace, before life had to start teaching her about the world so she could find her way back to love …

- Remember how she loved to colour, paint and sculpt
- Remember how she would imagine she was a member of the Famous Five or the mystery-solving Trixie Belden
- Remember how she would take her friends on adventures all over the countryside
- Remember how she would create hair and make-up styles on her Fashion Face Barbie
- Remember how she loved board-game nights
- Remember how she would fossick in rock pools and make 'biscuits' out of sand
- Remember how she would dream of Christmas Day stockings
- Remember how she would play games of Marco Polo in her friend's swimming pool
- Remember how she loved games of spotlight

My memories of childhood peace and contentment are endless, and I wish they had continued into my adult years. I was truly blessed and privileged and I know not all childhoods are this way—I wish they were.

What 'rememberings' can take you back to your peace in childhood, and help bring it back into today?

My hope is that once we successfully receive our life lessons and get free of everything in the way of our peace and love, we can regain some semblance of our childlike innocence, peace and contentment.

MESSAGE FOR YOUR PATH TO LOVE

Peace is a superpower; a most deeply desired state, even if this is unacknowledged. Our self-care and our self-love provide the portal to our peace, the state we most deserve. From our peace, all else flows. Life unfolds with more grace and ease. Even amidst chaos, we can reach within and connect with our peace, and in so doing tap into our reserves of love.

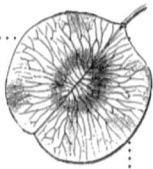

SELF-CARE IDEA FOR TODAY

Use *Pearls of Wisdom: For Your Path to Peace* as an oracle. Ask, *What steps do I need to take to regain my inner peace?* Open the book and receive the guidance you most need on this day.

I'VE GOT THIS, BUT DO I REALLY?

There is a part of you that knows you have what it takes; access it now.

It seems to be part of the human condition that no matter how successful we are, or how much we are showing up for ourselves or others, there is a little part inside (our protective ego voice) that wants to challenge this. In recent years, I have heard this process referred to as imposter syndrome. It is that place where we question, *Who am I to be doing this*, or *writing this*, or *creating this*, or *saying this?* It can come into play in expected and unexpected scenarios: it has a tricky dynamic. It may occur if we compare ourselves and our work unfavourably with another; or if we have been lax with our self-care to the point of overwhelm; or when we are working so hard but have had little acknowledgement for our work, and can't really perceive the fruits of our labour ... yet.

It would appear that most of us sensitive, spiritual types have a version of this syndrome that rears up every now and then. It is designed to test us and to ultimately make us reconnect with and recommit to our chosen path or mission with renewed confidence, trust, belief and optimism. I believe these moments of self-doubt are born from our love: a deep desire to make a difference in the world.

What the world requires from light workers (yes, that's you, or you wouldn't be reading this book) can feel so overwhelming at times that we give in to moments of doubt, almost as a reprieve from our work. That is more than okay. We can't have our light switched on intensely all the time—we do need to recharge or at least use the dimmer switch as required. The overwhelm shows up with us questioning, *Can I really do this? Is this really what life is requiring of me?* The answer is yes, yes, yes. You've answered the call and you would not be on this path, completing your missions or divine assignments if you did not have what it takes. Life does not present to us what we aren't equipped to handle. You were born for this.

Be kind to yourself when moments of uncertainty regarding your potential arrive. We have big tasks at hand, and these require our large, loving heart and beautiful self-care to centre us back into our belief and purpose.

Confidence is key and it is learned. Self-confidence is an art that requires our commitment to catching our breaking-down thoughts and turning them into building-up thoughts. At the same time, we need to be allowing of the myriad of emotions that can swirl within us when we are stepping up and showing up for ourselves and others. Up-levelling often requires more visibility and being heard in ways that may not be our preferred style. Many of us prefer to be quiet achievers, working diligently and effectively in the background and avoiding the spotlight. Sometimes, as part of our chosen path, the spotlight finds us. During these times, imposter syndrome can surface, but we can lovingly settle it back down by reminding ourselves that we have got this, Universe has our back, our path is guided and supported, we deserve success and abundance, and all is ultimately well. We need to develop our own personal confidence-building script around all of this. We can become the best coach ever.

Imposter syndrome often occurs for me just before a large breakthrough, or when I take a pivot in my pathway, or before an exciting opportunity, or before a new project or idea wishes to be born through me into the world. In this sense, imposter syndrome can be a form of resistance to what we are calling in next; the forthcoming potential and the up-levelling of us. What better way to handle this than to be still and calm, step back and ask, *How can love lead the way here?* Surrender to the greatness of you and to the love that flows within you and all around you. It's time to say: 'Imposter syndrome begone. You are on notice. You are longer needed. I have great work to do. I know who I am and what I am here for. I am unstoppable.'

MESSAGE FOR YOUR PATH TO LOVE

Belief in ourselves and our work is fuelled by confidence and love. Love means nurturing, caring, kindness, compassion, hope, trust, joy and receiving. **Our confidence develops by directing love in all its forms to ourselves.** It doesn't matter how often someone else tells us how amazing we are; we need to train ourselves to believe in ourselves enough that this desired state becomes a part of our natural default system, rather than something that only occurs fleetingly.

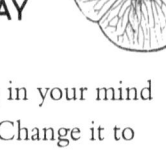

SELF-CARE IDEA FOR TODAY

Rewrite the script that is currently running in your mind about your potential in your chosen area. Change it to one that is uplifting and supportive of your dreams and intentions.

JEWELLERY

You are priceless. Adorn yourself with jewels as precious as you are.

Jewellery is self-care because it provides an instant mood elevation as our senses perceive, receive, and connect with the beauty before us. Jewellery provides sparkles and living light, love and energy to carry with us throughout our days.

Opening a jewellery box is an invitation to experience wonder, awe and love as we perceive the beauty and exquisite creations before us. Our jewellery boxes contain little pieces of heaven in the form of precious metals and gemstones interwoven to create unique expressions of craftsmanship and creativity.

A large array of metals, crystals and gemstones have healing and protective qualities: self-care in action. For example, silver is great for deflecting negative energies and gold has healing properties.

If a piece of jewellery feels good to wear—regardless of whether it is homemade or purchased—we are indulging in a loving act towards self. Acknowledge that you are wearing a little gift, a form of priceless creativity, around your neck. Connect with Earth elements and the energy of creativity as these beautiful pieces are brought to life.

Jewellery is an invitation to step into that elevated state of love known as gratitude. How did we get so lucky to have beautiful things to adorn and nurture our body and soul with? How blessed are we that someone has taken the time to select a piece of jewellery and gift it to us? Honour the memories associated with receiving gifts of jewellery.

Connect also with the love that shines through jewellery that has been created by devoted artisans. Just like us, every gemstone or precious metal has a journey and has been chosen by many along the way before it reaches you. Appreciate the crafting of each special piece. Creativity is love in action.

MESSAGE FOR YOUR PATH TO LOVE

Jewellery contains the energy of love—often we have fallen in love with a particular piece before we have even purchased it. Often, jewellery is gifted to us from those we love, for very special occasions, so therein lies beautiful energy that we get to hold with us throughout our days. Remember how special you are by wearing your best jewellery for any occasion, on any day. You deserve prince or princess royal days whenever you so desire.
You are worth it.

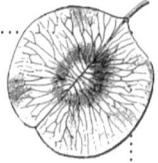

SELF-CARE IDEA FOR TODAY

Cherish yourself enough to start creating your very own treasure chest of jewellery. You are a treasure, and you deserve it.

JOURNALLING

Unlock your magic and wisdom through your pen and paper.

Journalling is a most personal, vulnerable and powerful form of self-care. It helps us to unpack and unload our feelings, and move out of overthinking and into our heart awareness. Through journalling, we lessen the emotional charge and desperation often associated with strong emotions. It helps us to pinpoint our truth, to know what is truly going on within, to understand our triggers and move beyond them. We become our own nurturers, our best healers.

Journalling helps us to clear away our mental and emotional clutter, and reveal our own breathtakingly amazing pure wisdom. It helps us to see different perspectives around what we may be experiencing and perceiving. We can connect with our subconscious, which is trying to rise to the surface to assist us with our truth seeking. We find more and more of our truths each time we put pen to paper.

Our self-worth grows through journalling because we come to know ourselves more intimately and at the same time move away from judgement of ourselves and into respect and even awe. No-one else is involved other than ourselves and our connection with our higher power. The very act of taking out our pen and journal, combined with creating the space for stillness and reflection, opens us to our intuition, divine guidance and deep, innate wisdom. This is a very enlightening combination.

Journalling allows us to release onto paper anything that is weighing heavily upon our soul. It is deeply cathartic and healing as it releases emotional responses before they become deeply entrenched in our psyches or become harmful stories that we play on autopilot.

Journalling allows us a personal reset. It takes us from a moment, or a position, or an energy we may be stuck in, to a state of grace. It unburdens us from things we may have taken on from others; we often automatically decide that if we feel unease, it must be ours—then often judge that there is something wrong with us and our choices. We learn to move towards seeking the truth rather than hiding like mushrooms in our own darkness. Journalling forces us into the light—our true home. It allows the ego part of our mind to stay quiet so that we can hear the voice of our own guidance, intuition and wisdom. It is soul soothing and deeply comforting as we step into a powerful space of our own making.

Journalling encourages us to become a living question and opens us to the wisdom of the Universe. We are in a state of surrender as we let go of control, suspend judgement, and receive wisdom that arises from a place outside of our small human selves; we connect with our super selves. In this space, we can dissipate stress and anxiety and enhance our immune system with greater ease.

Any time I feel heaviness or anything in my body that is not peace, I seek clarity and my own truth through journalling. I usually start with the following types of questions.

Dear guidance team:

- What is this heaviness I am experiencing?
- What is right about this I am not getting?
- What is triggering me?
- What do I need to release to move forward?
- What can I let go of to step into my power?
- What do I need to release here that is causing unease?

- What am I unwilling or unable to perceive here?
- What is going on with …?
- What is my reaction to … all about?
- What am I resisting that I need to be embracing for my highest good?

MESSAGE FOR YOUR PATH TO LOVE

Open your journal to open to the love that is within. You are getting to know you on a very deep and truthful level, which is perfect self-care. Let your vulnerable outpourings connect you with your deep, innate wisdom and guidance.

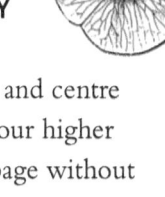

SELF-CARE IDEA FOR TODAY

Be still, be quiet, be present. Breathe deeply and centre yourself. Now open your journal and ask your higher self a question. Let the words flow onto the page without engaging with them until you reach the end. Have gratitude and reverence for all that is revealed by you, for you.

KAIROS TIME

Soar when it's time to soar and flow when it's time to flow.

Chronos is the biblical word for the time of day in terms of hours, minutes and seconds. Kairos means in nature's time or due time. There is a divine order to kairos time. Chronos or 'clock time' is essential for navigating the human world. However, if we become relentlessly fixed on our plans and deadlines, we can miss out on flow and opportunity that can come outside of linear time and may only exist beyond our control. Kairos time allows us to step more into divine timing as we surrender our fixation on set outcomes. It involves more 'right time' or opportune timing. It is not a passive approach. We act as we are intuitively guided, from a place where something greater than our logical mind can step in. We are more powerful in this space, oftentimes creating and attracting more with seemingly less effort.

Being attuned with our self-care needs and to where we are situated with our connection to love allows us to release fear-based control and move into surrender. We can go with the flow and act on opportunities and situations that we may not have considered when aligning completely with chronos time. We move away from the stance of *I must do this now, and then this, and then that*, with no deviation or flexibility. When we embrace kairos time, we seem to be more in sync with the seasons and cycles of life. Unexpected life events and challenges cease to derail us to the same degree. We give up resisting what is occurring and the associated turmoil and move into the power of presence and acceptance. We trust that we are in the right place and time for our highest good.

New thinking and new solutions arise out of our connection with kairos time. Chronos time is often associated with a lack of spontaneity and repetitive, almost autopilot routines and behaviours. Creativity arises more when flowing with kairos timing. Patience is essential to access kairos time; knowing that we will get where we need or desire to be, all in good time.

Self-care and serenity help us to access kairos time. Kairos time is found in the space where we step out of linear *(I am governed by time)* to a space that is seamless, flowing, creative and present. For me, kairos time arises out of the present moment, out of stillness, where I'm led into a different space of being, flowing and creating each day.

We are led by kairos time when we intuitively listen to the call to act. This may be to write, or to go to this place for dinner, or to do our groceries or to head into our garden. It's like Universe leading the dance of our lives rather than us. It's larger than time as we know it. In this time, we are always where we need to be, doing what we need to be doing for our highest good.

I have found the more time I spend honouring myself and my care, the more time expands for me. I get way more done with less effort and with greater enjoyment.

> *'Giving yourself time is the same as giving yourself love. Start by recognising that you deserve to operate from a fully charged battery, and then go about the business of charging it.'*
> — Alan Cohen

MESSAGE FOR YOUR PATH TO LOVE

Kairos is her own boss and will ensure you arrive right on time for all your dates with destiny. Whenever you can, let go and just be. Surrender to what is occurring around you, follow your intuition and act accordingly with divine timing as your compass.

SELF-CARE IDEA FOR TODAY

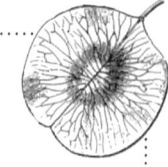

Declare your next day off from formal work as a kairos time day. Start the day without any plan or to-do list. Breathe and tune into your intuition and follow what you feel like doing and where you are called to go. Stay in the moment and allow your heart to take you where it desires to take you.

LAUGHTER

*Laughter is powerful medicine
for body and soul.*

Laughter is an instant vibration raiser and is one of the simplest, most effective acts of self-care. The energy of love courses through our veins during vigorous bouts of laughter as we are celebrating the joy of life.

Through laughter, we become more optimistic and hopeful. A great laugh brings us directly into the powerful present moment. Laughter mutes negative thinking and emotions. It allows us to be lighthearted and childlike, and transforms serious, responsible moments into those more pleasurable.

The effects of laughter can stay with us throughout the day, reducing our stress levels, shifting stuck energies, providing a direct connection to the love within us, and radiating light to all those around us.

Every cell in our bodies feels the energy of our laughter. Laughter really is the best medicine as it is an immediate endorphin producer and emotion elevator. Our minds are given the opportunity to let go of any current limiting thoughts before there is a corresponding emotional response in our bodies.

Laugh as often and as hard as you can, anytime, anywhere.

Humour is a beautiful connector to others. We love being around those who make us laugh. Laughter gives permission for others to lighten up along with you. Comedians and humorous people are such an incredible gift to us and the world. We become brighter, happier and more alert after a good dose of humour.

What could bring you laughter and elevate your emotions

today? Perhaps it could be:

- Reading funny literature
- Watching a hilarious movie
- Being around others who are laughing—it's so infectious in a great way!
- Catching up with a witty friend and connecting and conversing in person
- Finding things funny that we really shouldn't find funny …
- Listening to people share crazy and weird experiences
- Funny memes and posts
- The conversations of children
- Just starting to laugh for no reason
- Enjoying lots of flirtatious repartee with a loved one
- Prank shows
- Strange noises
- Wardrobe malfunctions
- Fancy-dress parties
- Funny home videos when things go a tad wrong
- Getting up to mischief and playing with your children
- Watching the antics of pets and animals

MESSAGE FOR YOUR LOVE TO IGNITE

The wonderful thing about laughter is that it can be found often and anywhere if we are open to it, and we keep the desire for it constantly on our radar. Basically, anywhere and anytime you find fun and frivolity can provide a doorway to laughter. It is one of the most accessible and inexpensive forms of self-care and self-love.

SELF-CARE IDEA FOR TODAY

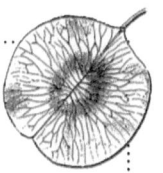

Make a commitment to bring laughter into **this day** as much as you can. You will be gifting yourself instant, beautiful self-care and love.

LETTER TO YOUR SWEET YOUNGER SELF FROM YOUR HIGHER SELF

Your higher self knows you and loves you better than any self.

One of the most loving acts we can do for ourselves is to acknowledge the enormity of the journey that we have undertaken through life on Earth, aka boot camp. Writing a letter to our younger self from our higher self celebrates all the wisdom, healing and compassion we have bravely acquired. It acknowledges the deep complexity and powerful nature of our divinity. We are reminded that we are spiritual beings having a highly personal human experience, designed perfectly for us—even when at times it most certainly does not feel this way.

This process of writing connects us with an even deeper wisdom and intuition. It allows our deep vulnerability and gratitude to be witnessed, which in themselves are acts of great self-love.

For me, opening to this letter surprised me in innumerable ways. I am humbled by the divine workings supporting our whole life experience, as I know you will be too when you let the light shine on your own journey up to today.

I applaud and congratulate you. You are and will continue to make a difference. You are amazingness in action.

Dearest Jane,
I know all you wanted to do as a young girl was play and fit in, but you weren't born to fit in, and life had bigger

plans for you than just playing. You were meant to lead, shine, create and transform yourself and others. This path is never easy as it can be a lonely way. It is difficult to find true connection, not because you are not enough, but often because you are too much of what others don't understand. You've always had a mission, a purpose to activate in this life, and that required life to present to you great obstacles to learn from and to overcome so that you could show others the way.

Your life has been one of great contrasts: unbridled joy, amazing opportunities, great love, adventure, abundance, and success, combined with a deeply challenging excavation of your own limiting shadow aspects, life lessons, and karma. The challenges you've endured made the way for *Pearls of Wisdom: For Your Path to Peace* to be born into the world and we thank you for that.

You have so beautifully come to understand through this tumultuous process of life that the greatest battle individuals have is with themselves. Peace on Earth begins within every individual.

Your process of emerging has allowed you to show others the way—through your business, writing and presence.

You have learnt not to worry, as worry is a waste of energy that keeps problems circulating on repeat. You have learnt that it does not matter what others think of you, and that fretting over this is how we keep ourselves small and limited. You have learnt that life and oneself evolve in their fullness only through looking truthfully within and at the same time embracing nourishment through self-care and self-love. You have learnt that when you have love for self, the right people, designed perfectly for you, eventually show up for you and love you right back—and help you to expand into even greater levels of wholeness.

You have learnt that every ounce of love, care and guidance you have ever shown and gifted to your children has come back to you tenfold in a myriad of unexpected ways. Being a mother is a great act of service, and when we serve others, the Universe serves us back.

You have learnt that giving up control and embracing stillness, surrender, flow and the beautiful unknown is where the true magic, synchronicity, wonder, awe and possibility of life arises and arises and arises. You have at last learnt to be not so hard on yourself: great intent and purpose must be balanced with deep compassion, love and gratitude for all one has been and will continue to become. You know the evolving is never complete and you have embraced this and handed over the reins.

We've got this, you've got this—co-creation at its best.

What else is calling for you to bring forth? Are you ready for some explosive changes?

The last part of the letter did challenge me somewhat as I've always preferred change of a gentler nature—that I can adjust to with minimal duress. Maybe I'm ready for more than I perceive I'm ready for …

Universe doesn't give us what we can't handle, so time to step it up again, Jane Elizabeth!

MESSAGE FOR YOUR PATH TO LOVE

Quiet the ego and connect with the powerful, uplifting and caring wisdom of your higher self. You will function in life with greater peace, potential and power.

SELF-CARE IDEA FOR TODAY

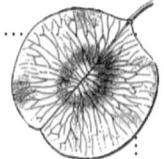

Find a quiet place, a beautiful notebook and a gorgeous pen. Ask your higher self what it would like your younger self to know. Breathe and receive your beautiful letter.

LIGHTEN UP

Enjoy things that are not meant to be funny ... or are they?

One of the things that I most enjoy about myself is my ability to see the funny side of things—particularly things that are often not meant to be funny. Such occurrences have often been considered too 'inappropriate' to be funny.

I soon learned this about myself in childhood but tended to squash it to a certain degree to keep myself out of trouble. The incident that comes to mind was a church experience late in primary school. My mother used to like us to go along to church on Christmas Eve. The 'seriousness' of church often proved to be a disaster on the laughing front for my father and me. One time, there was a man in front of us who would sing the hymns in a very robust way, with great gusto. We were singing a song called 'Rejoice' and this gentleman worked up splendiferous rolling Rs at each singing of the word rejoice. It was the literal undoing of my dad and me! That feeling of it being absolutely inappropriate to laugh had us in fits of 'trying to contain it' laughter. We were shaking from top to toe. What made it worse was that my mum (who was sitting in between us) was horrified and kept elbowing us in the ribs, harshly whispering, '*Don, Jane, stop it!*'

I realised as I got older that attempts to fit in and to be always socially acceptable didn't involve me being particularly true to myself, so I gave it up. I believe owning what we find funny is a way to reclaim our childlike responses to life, to lighten up and to not take ourselves or life events too seriously. This is a great act of self-love and self-care. Avoid allowing society or anyone else to dictate what you find funny. It is a unique response for us all, a true gift from our souls.

The idea for this chapter came through in the middle of the night when I couldn't stop laughing about a scenario I had with my husband's best friend and his dog. Without 'processing' too much what I was about to say, I made a comment about his British bulldog being kind of ugly in a really cute sort of way. I learned quickly that you don't say this kind of thing to a British bulldog owner! I did send him a Facebook invite to an event called 'Bulldogs are Beautiful Day' in an attempt to make up for it. Cue more laughter! Suffice to say the banter that went on around this was priceless and I still to this day cannot stop laughing whenever I think about it.

This friend is coming to visit us tomorrow and he texted my husband to let me know that he and his ugly dog would be around late morning. My first greeting tomorrow will be along the lines of how handsome his dog is looking, and that he's got more attractive as he has got older. I know the laughter and stirring marathon will begin again. I'm ready!

There are countless times where I have felt the urge to laugh, when perhaps I should not have. In staff meetings, when certain individuals would get worked up and heated, I would feel a dose of giggles coming on and have to rapidly excuse myself to the bathroom for a good 'laugh off' before returning. I also think by now I should have grown out of finding certain bodily noises funny, but no … and it's often the louder the better. One time, in cooking class, a friend asked me to check on her cake and I let go of the oven door too hard. Unfortunately, it flopped in the middle and was no longer a possible pride and joy for her. That was the absolute end of us both in class; unstoppable laughter was the only thing we were making for the rest of the lesson.

Another time, I was walking through a shopping centre with my friend and suddenly she disappeared down a worker's manhole, with only her head and shoulders visible. Only her pride was hurt as she was effortlessly hoisted out by the workers—but I was in hysterics.

As well as giving ourselves permission to laugh whenever it arises, we also need to be able to laugh at ourselves: at all our not-so-perfect moments (aren't they just the best?) and our quirks and foibles. I acquired this trait in high school when we were learning to cross-stitch, and I inadvertently sewed my needlework to my school dress. Another time, at the movies, something jumped out on the screen and I let out a bloodcurdling scream, and no-one else did! My children were horrified and sunk into their seats, and that sent me into a crescendo of laughter.

MESSAGE FOR YOUR LOVE TO FLOURISH

Laughing at ourselves is beautiful self-care because we are free of the need to be perfect, to impress others, or to behave in certain ways to gain approval. We are worth more than crushing our spirit and who we are in a misguided attempt to fit in.

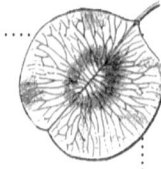

SELF-CARE IDEA FOR TODAY

Reminisce over some of the things you have experienced that you found funny—that perhaps, given the situation, you should not have found amusing. Share these stories with others to create a super-healing laughter festival.

MONEY AND PROSPERITY

Care for your money and allow it to care for you.

Money is the energy of freedom. We love the freedom to be, do, have and create whenever and whatever we choose. It allows us to care for ourselves in as many ways as we would like. (Luckily, there are a plethora of self-care opportunities and ways of gifting and receiving that don't have any cost involved.)

Money is a blessing and can be a currency of love and self-care. Money enables us to provide for ourselves the traditional types of self-care that require payment. It is a form of nurturing ourselves and gifting to ourselves those things that light us up, including self-care.

Money provides a way of reciprocal receiving. We give love in the form of financial support to the person providing us with a service—and they get to contribute to our care in turn. Serving others is a way to demonstrate love.

We can change the realities of others with money: we all have people, causes and organisations that we love to support. There is nothing better than gifting to others and seeing and perceiving the joy in their universes.

Money can't buy happiness, but it can provide us with more opportunities to enhance our health and wellbeing and assist with the care of others.

Being responsible with our money is a form of self-care as it can allow us to create a little nest egg that makes us feel provided for and powerful. When we have a financial buffer zone, we always feel cared for by ourselves and safe during times when life throws unexpected curve balls like the large one we all received in 2020. Closing my business for four months certainly was a personal reminder to have money in reserve.

The amount we require in reserve to feel comfortable will vary for us all and depend on our current earning capacity. It may be five hundred dollars, one thousand, two thousand, five thousand, ten thousand or beyond. There will be a figure that will be just right for you and take into consideration your circumstances.

A nest egg will make you feel more valuable than you may imagine. Sometimes, spending a few nest eggs is required to really value having one. The contrast between feeling light and free with money and wondering if we can make ends meet is often enough motivation for us to make the demand of ourselves to never 'go there' again by being reckless with our funds. Having to scrimp and scrounge for dollars does not add to our self-worth.

Work with your budget, but also put something away every payday as a gift to you. Balance is key. Spending within your means honours you and your money. Credit-card debt can feel like a black, low-vibe cloud, which then tunes us into feeling guilty for not better managing our money. The opposite of this—knowing you can have what you want, when you want it (even if you have no intention of spending)—is so liberating, empowering and confidence boosting, and is therefore first-class self-care. Credit cards generate the energy of poverty rather than prosperity—unless managed expertly.

Even if we're existing pay cheque to pay cheque, our financial situation can change in a heartbeat. Believe that you can have financial abundance as your potential reality.

During one of my 'not feeling so financially sound' times, I slipped into a kind of peaceful melancholy over my current money status quo. I was fine with my situation, but at the same time I desired so much more of myself. This was mainly because I perceive that our ability to receive money reflects our self-worth and the beliefs we have around deservedness—and is indicative of our ability to receive in general.

When contemplating the writing of this chapter, I was sitting on my garden swing, pondering my current financial status. I felt 'abundant' in life and within. However, because my husband was earning so much more than me, I didn't feel I was contributing enough. Now, I perceive that, energetically, I was contributing to everything he was creating too. He would always say it's a 'we' not a 'you and I' and that 'what's mine is yours', etc. However, I wanted to feel proud of my own ability to generate.

As I was mulling this over, three things happened simultaneously that are signs of receiving and prosperity for me: a dragonfly flew back and forth in front of me; a butterfly flew to the side of me; and—blessing of all blessings and a true sign of impending abundance—a beautiful ladybird landed on my arm. Tears of gratitude and awe welled in my eyes. I knew I was loved by Universe and that my silent prayer for a sign that the seeds I'd been planting would bloom soon had been answered. I felt that financial prosperity was on its way for me in divine timing for my highest good.

Love and two of its derivatives, gratitude and joy, provide powerful fuel for money and prosperity. These states help us to choose abundance rather than lack and fear. We can make the choice for abundance daily: the more we choose joy, the more we are choosing money. Have gratitude for everything—it's the highest form of currency and draws more to us, such is the magnetic attraction between gratitude and receiving. There is no limit to what we can receive. The more we have, the more we can gift to others, creating a beautiful ebb and flow, just like the tides. We do limits; Universe does not.

Thank Universe in advance for the money that is coming: like when placing an order at a restaurant, trust it will be delivered.

Select some great affirmations to enhance your money flows:

- I tune into and become the high-vibrational frequency of money
- I am a magnet for money
- Success and abundance flow to me continually
- When I flow money out, money flows in
- Money is always flowing to me in both expected and unexpected ways
- I focus on the love that surrounds me and draw in money miracles
- I have good fortune
- I trust that abundance and financial prosperity beyond my wildest dreams are on their way for me
- I am wealthy in my own right and so worthy of it

Changing our points of view around money enhances our money flows. Identify where you may be duplicating the points of view of your family or fostering your own limiting beliefs. It may be unconsciously believing things like: *Money doesn't grow on trees, Money doesn't make us happy, It takes money to make money, The rich get richer and the poor get poorer, I will never have any money, Money slips through my fingers, I spend every cent I earn, I may as well spend it because I can't take it with me.* The list is endless, and we unconsciously 'buy' these points of view from those around us and make them real for us. Unfortunately, they impact our choices and our beliefs around what is possible for us. Change the beliefs of your family lineage and create positive points of view around money.

These are some monetary points of view that have helped me:

- Money is fun, adventurous and awe-inspiring
- Money can arrive in an instant, from anywhere, at any

time
- I am worthy of receiving success and financial prosperity
- My great work deserves to be championed, received and rewarded

MESSAGE FOR YOUR PATH TO LOVE

What we all require is more wisdom and love (true prosperity) as opposed to money. Wisdom and love help us to access our inner guidance, power and creativity. From here, we can successfully draw financial prosperity to us with far greater ease. Money can then serve and uplift us, not control us.

If we haven't taken care of our inner world, money may either become our master or evaporate before our eyes—as we are subconsciously unwilling to receive.

Money is a form of energy. High-vibrational energetic states are created within—magnetically enabling us to attract more and to actually enjoy the gifts we receive.

SELF-CARE IDEA FOR TODAY

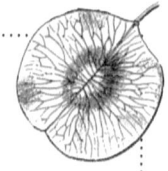

Try these money tips:
- Hoarding can limit our money flows. Release things you no longer require and free up some energy. Creating a void allows for something new to flow in.
- Look carefully at your motivations for purchasing things. Breathe and tune into your energy before making purchases. If it feels light and expansive (with no guilt attached) to purchase, then do so. Enjoy your gift to self and allow it to light you up and make you feel beautiful.
- Avoid shopping when bored. Do something creative instead. Over-consuming can be a sign of attempting to stifle our creativity or numbing ourselves to what is going on within us or in life.

MUSIC

*Music is an instant mood elevator:
straight to the top floor.*

Music is magic for our souls and an accessible, simple form of self-care. It can soothe, uplift and inspire us. Music has the power to invoke any mood we would like to experience. Go inward with your music and allow it to speak to your heart. Listen mindfully and experience the whispers of wisdom that it can unlock within. Let music heal every cell in your body with the joy that is infused through the weaving of sounds and lyrics.

Songs hold memories. Allow music to unearth beautiful memories of people, experiences and places.

Music infuses us with creative energy. I find ideas for writing often drop into my mind while I'm immersed in a tune or two. Music without lyrics can set beautiful background moods conducive to relaxation. It can also help us to drown out distracting thoughts and focus positively on what is required.

Music can be our guide—a way Universe can connect with us, pass on information and gift to us love. I regularly awaken to song lyrics playing in my head. I pause and reflect on what messages may be coming through for me via songs. Days before I secured a publishing deal for my first book, I heard the Roxette song lyric, *living in a box but thats's when opportunity nox*. Being in lockdown at the time, I did feel quite boxed in, and opportunity certainly knocked. I eagerly answered her call.

More encouraging song lyrics that have played in my mind are *Here is the rainbow I've been praying for, it's gonna be a bright, bright, sunshiny day … I can see all obstacles in my way* from Johnny Nash's

'I Can See Clearly Now'.

On another occasion, whilst travelling in my car, I was pondering my future direction as an author. I was wondering what it might look like for me, what would light me up most and what I might be called to do. Moments later, the Fleetwood Mac song 'Go Your Own Way' came on the radio. Then, almost immediately after that, I pulled up behind a ute that had a sign saying Go Your Own Way. I did not need to adopt any set approach, just follow my own intuition and go my own way even if I didn't currently have a roadmap.

There are specific songs that have a powerful and unique effect on each of us. Discover your songs: in so doing, care for you and feel the love within that they conjure.

Some that come to mind for me that you may also enjoy are as follows:

- Kelsea Ballerini's music—I almost float out of my body with the lilt of her tunes.
- 'Paint' by Roxette takes me back to the vibrancy and spirit of my teens.
- Roxette's 'Almost Unreal' is reminiscent of the love and connection I have with my husband.
- Anything from Kylie and I'm smiling.
- Keith Urban's songs uplift and infuse love into my cells—especially 'Won't Let You Down'.
- 'Romeo and Juliet' by Dire Straits connects me with that timeless, enduring, across-time love.
- 'I Fell in Love with the Devil' by Avril Lavigne reminded me of the kind of love I did not want to be attracting (even if that was the case for a while).
- 'It was in Me' by Avril Lavigne is a reminder that love, power, wisdom and peace are found within—and that life will conspire to help us find it, if we stay open for it.

- 'You're the Voice' by John Farnham assisted me to adopt my 'get writing, girl' stance.
- The opening bar of Faith Hill's 'Lost' elevates me instantly.
- 'Brave New Girl' by Britney Spears connected me with being willing to be seen and heard, even though that felt highly uncomfortable for me.
- 'Show Yourself' from *Frozen 2* reminds me that I am the one I've *been waiting for ... all of my life.*
- John Lennon's 'Imagine' encourages my belief in a greater world.

MESSAGE FOR YOUR PATH TO LOVE

I love musical signs and the feelings, memories and thoughts that specific songs bring to my awareness. Words and lyrics are such a powerful combination. Allow music to assist the love that is already within you to bloom and flourish.

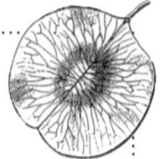

SELF-CARE IDEA FOR TODAY

Compile a list of snippets from song lyrics that have called to you: those that nurture and uplift you. Read through them when you need reminding of how special you are. Create a soothing self-care playlist for listening

NATURE

Just as nature can regenerate and transform under the right conditions, so too can we.

Nature calls to us, nurtures us and nourishes us. During these somewhat tumultuous and stressful times, many of us are starting to remember just how much we thrive in nature. Our healing parasympathetic nervous system is activated, and fight-or-flight adrenal functioning is quietened with each moment mindfully absorbed in nature. We heal when we are calm and free of excess stress hormones. We are beginning to reconnect with the healing properties and wisdom of nature. Nature is a beautiful combination of power and peace—a duo that creates much change and transformation. We can embrace these qualities and bloom through our own self-care, opening the doorway to our inner love.

Immerse yourself in nature to soothe your soul and to shift stagnant emotions, anxiety, and fear. We need her more than we can imagine. She elevates our emotions and teaches us to connect with wonder and awe. Being in a state of wonder and awe is direct evidence that we are connecting with love. Mother Nature has many lessons and life analogies for us if we follow her lead, and embrace the seasons and cycles of life.

In nature, there is a season for everything. Just as flowers have their unique, specifically chosen times to bloom, so often do we—we can't force things into being. Just like in nature, we need restoration to prepare for the next blooming. The flourishing of us seems even more perfect after quieter, more dormant times—times when much is happening with the seeds we have planted below the surface. Embrace and flow with your seasonal flowerings.

> 'You should sit in nature for twenty minutes a day …
> unless you're busy, then you should sit for an hour.'
> — Zen saying

Nature's vistas and views (whether they be those in front of us or those we connect with via images) can inspire and heal us from afar. Mountain views, desertscapes and tropical paradise scenes have the power to change our energy, mood, and thought patterns. Each vista can invoke different feelings within us. Tune into whatever vista makes you feel peace, contentment or any desired emotion your self-care requires.

We can absorb the energy of a location simply by witnessing it. Where would your heart and soul like to experience today? Focus on how you want to feel before making your selection.

Soak up new vistas as often as possible to leave the predictable behind and embrace the unknown. A change of scenery changes our thinking. Changing our thinking allows us to become a changed person. New vistas allow us to reset and rewire into greater potential as we and our lives are not running on autopilot.

> 'Pay attention to episodes in nature that … kindle an inner spark of awe
> and admiration for you. You don't have to discuss it with another being—
> if it has meaning to you, it's valid.'
> — Dr Wayne Dyer

Nature invokes our natural creativity and is our greatest muse. The beauty of nature inspires all forms of creativity. She helps our true selves to emerge as we are cared for and nourished by the natural energies and the ever-flowing beauty that surrounds us.

Every cell in our bodies is impacted by the song of nature. She is a great awakener—helping us to emerge from the dream that we are separate from the earthly realm. We are intrinsically linked to all the wonders that abound in the natural world. Let old patterns fall away as the autumn leaves fall. Breathe in fresh air to cleanse and enliven. Enjoy bathing in the warmth of the sun and plunge into the sea to emerge cleansed and invigorated.

Nature helps to quieten our mind so we can hear the voice of our intuition and connect with our heart. We feel balanced, grounded and centered after time in nature.

Attune to the vibration of the bees and become enchanted by birdsong. Become immersed in the dappled and varied shades of green in leaves dancing under the sun. Hug a tree to feel comforted and strong as you connect with Mother Earth through strong roots. Miracles abound in nature, from the delicate, artistically created patterns and spirals in shells, to the unique, exquisite designs of snowflakes.

Witness and observe miracles in nature as a starting point for observing and attracting them in your own life.

Nature provides mindfulness and meditation opportunities. We have all felt the calming, comforting, mesmerising effects of sitting in front of a fire.

Fire is symbolic of burning away low vibrational energies and stances. It is resonant of transmuting what is no longer needed—reminiscent of the phoenix rising from the ashes in greater glory and power. Be present and let go of thinking as you focus on the beauty, power and chakra-clearing red of the coals, the movement of the flames, and the soothing warmth radiating from the fire. When witnessing the little sparks, ask *What little sparks of insight can I have today?* Remember your power when meditating in front of a fire: it only takes a spark to light a fire.

Just as we contain much treasure within (waiting to be discovered), so too does Mother Earth. She has a treasure trove of precious crystals deep within, awaiting our discovery.

Crystals are blessings of beauty. They are gifts from the earth, containing all the power, magic and secrets of the earth. Crystals are transmitters of information, light, wisdom and healing and can be used in a variety of ways as part of our self-care.

We can create affirmations around specific crystals and their properties. For example, rose quartz is synonymous with love, so we could say, 'I connect with the love that is within me and all around me.'

Befriend crystals for certain experiences, intentions and moments in time. They are little friends that will always be there for us, providing unconditional love in the form of healing and awakening.

A beautiful self-care ritual is to visit a crystal shop and see which ones call to you. If specific colours or vibrations call to you, then they will be what you and your body most require.

I find I am particularly drawn to crystals during winter. I require their energy as I'm not receiving as much from the sun or nature. I love sunstone during winter for its radiance and ability to invoke joy. Citrine is great for generating abundance, selenite for creating high-vibrational spaces, black tourmaline for clearing negative energies and protecting our energies, rose quartz for connecting with love, and lapis lazuli for helping us find our voice. Amethyst is great for connecting us with our intuition.

Nature communicates with us and often provides great analogies and wisdom for living in harmony. On my launch day for *Pearls of Wisdom: For Your Path to Peace*, Universe provided me and everyone in the room with an analogy for living to embrace. Outside the room, the winds were blowing with ferocity and the seas were tumultuously rough. Inside, we were warm and peaceful, and the room was glowing with love. It provided a reminder for me that nothing outside of us truly has any power over us—we have all the power within to preserve our peace.

Another analogy I use in *Pearls* is comparing the adversity and suffering that we endure in life (which often heralds our true beauty and greatness) with the abrasion required to produce a beautiful pearl within an oyster.

Have reverence and respect for all of nature. She is sacred and abundant in wonderment and beauty. Nature teaches us to embrace the cycles, tides and seasons of life and to flow with and cherish them. Connect with your love through nature. She will help you to traverse any dark realms into those of light and love.

MESSAGE FOR YOUR LOVE TO COME ALIVE

Connection with nature is an essential part of our self-care. She helps to clear our minds and release unwanted emotions and energies. Nature grounds us, quietens us and soothes our souls. We can embrace the seasons and cycles of life as nature does—rather than resisting what is occurring. We can go inward in winter to heal and replenish, ready to bloom with inspiration and motivation in spring. In summer, we can relax into the beauty and flow of life, and in autumn, we can let go of all that needs to fall away within us and around us.

In nature, there is a season for everything …
and you are everything.

SELF-CARE IDEA FOR TODAY

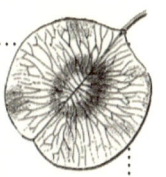

Embrace the natural world as a healer, energy clearer, balancer and uplifter. Allow yourself to be healed and nurtured by experiencing the brilliant life force emanating from everything.

Find a beautiful place in nature and go for a walk today. Allow Mother Nature to uplift you. With each step you take, imagine you are moving closer to the life you most want to live and to bringing forth the person you most aspire to be. Walking lets our souls know of our desire to move forward and to leave the past behind.

NETFLIX AND CHILL ... LITERALLY

Viewing time allows us the quiet time to balance all the go-do-it time.

Sometimes, my self-care is quite simply escapist TV, which vastly ranges in quality, depending on my mood. Sometimes I feel like a soap—*The Bold and the Beautiful* is my favourite decades-long habit—and on other occasions, beautiful, thought-provoking movies are required. It is such a brain break and a trip into realities of every description under the sun: many of which I wouldn't care to enter in my day-to-day existence. However, behind the safety and distance of a screen, it's all very 'acceptable' and fun. There's nothing to do but just sit and be entertained. Having a cup of tea in hand and a cosy couch elevates the experience to an even more relaxing and nurturing experience.

Like anything, too much of a good thing is not really a good thing. Balance is key, especially with Netflix, as one episode so beautifully and easily rolls into the next and the next.

I've only just discovered the world of Netflix. It began with a foray into *The Crown* and was followed by a love affair with the first season of *Bridgerton*. I don't anticipate my Netflix stage being a lengthy one as time is precious and television viewing can substantially erode this, but whilst in the depths of some heavy chapters for this book (some that were stirring up some things from my past to be healed) it was just what I needed. This demonstrates just how much our self-care needs shift and change according to what we are both experiencing and processing in our lives.

Our self-care requirements, just like our lives, are always in flux, and a large part of developing awareness and self-love is successfully tuning into this. We listen and act to deliver what we most require, now. We are ever-changeable beings.

Some days, a sunset or cleansing peaceful rain may soothe our soul, and on others, it might be an episode of alternate reality excess to the extreme. *Outlander, Game of Thrones* or your equivalent escapist, mind-distracting episode may be just the self-care hiatus from reality that you temporarily require. There are no rules with our self-care viewing needs; they are as individual and unique and as we are.

MESSAGE FOR YOUR PATH TO LOVE

> Self-care does not have to involve anyone else; it does not have to be costly, nor does it need to take place outside of your own home. Care and love do not have to be complicated. Simple self-care is often best and requires minimal effort for maximum results. Whatever form of self-care makes you feel good is also making you feel love.

SELF-CARE IDEA FOR TODAY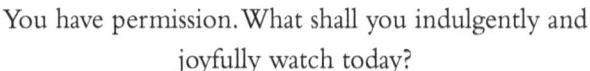

You have permission. What shall you indulgently and joyfully watch today?
Ask your friends to nominate their favourite series if you need a starting point. You will also get to have some bonding over common interests and shared joy.

NO EXPECTATIONS

Free yourself and others by releasing your expectations of them.

I've come to realise that a beautiful form of self-care and self-love (that has evolved within me over the years) is to place no expectations on anyone, other than myself. It has given me such freedom from reaction and has contributed to greater peace within and peace in life. Embracing a stance of no expectation means I am no longer the effect of anyone or anything. I am flowing, accepting, and allowing of what is occurring, as opposed to being vested in individuals behaving in ways that I have decided are most desirable for me. This was just another way that judging another could rear its (limiting, controlling, ego-dominated) head.

The way that having expectations can hurt us and hinder our development is if we project onto others how we think they should behave, treat us or respond to us. It involves quite a lot of judgement and control, as we have already 'decided' what we expect or require from another. When they don't 'deliver', we can be triggered and hurt. We can convince ourselves that we are justified in our hurt or upset when we tell ourselves that in that situation, we would have been there for them, or done this or that. Their responses and attitudes are completely theirs to own, and we don't have control over this and nor should we expect it. We aren't in someone else's shoes; we don't know their story, their background, their journey, or understand the events in life that have shaped them.

Looking through the eyes of love rather than fear helps us to accept 'what is' and allow others to be who they are currently choosing to be. People will only change if they want to or have the skills and awareness to do so. It is not up to us to instigate change for another unless our assistance and guidance are requested.

Being free of agendas is great not only in our relationships but also for life in general. Having no expectations around the dreams and visions that we have for our life (and how they show up for our highest good) is a caring and loving act. We put out into the Universe what we desire, we act according to our inner guidance, and then we release the need to be vested in set outcomes. We can then step into peace, acceptance, surrender and flow: all examples of love in action.

MESSAGE FOR YOUR PATH TO LOVE

Have gratitude for all the people who are showing up in your life exactly as they are. Focussing on the positive attributes of another brings forth more to celebrate. The opposite is also true: focussing on the things that we don't enjoy in another often encourages these behaviours to perpetuate. Our thoughts are that powerful, as where our attention goes, our energy flows.

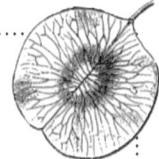

SELF-CARE IDEA FOR TODAY

Use the power of your mind to see only the positives within the people you associate with today. This is great self-care as feelings of peace will naturally arise from this state of being.

NO PROBLEM!

There are no problems; only opportunities for more questions and more growth.

Great self-care involves giving ourselves permission to feel good even if those around us are not choosing to feel good. It means becoming so comfortable with feeling good that we don't subconsciously create problems when there are none.

Sometimes, we feel safer being uncomfortable as we are afraid to feel good for long periods of time in case something happens to take it away from us. This 'something' is usually ourselves and our feelings of unworthiness (limiting our willingness to receive abundance in all its forms) or it could be that doubting ego voice that tells us *This is too good to be true.* There is a part within us that unconsciously prepares for the worst—just in case. This program needs to change to one of hoping for the best.

Avoid attempting to align or bond with others over 'problems'. There can be a tendency to manufacture problems to fit in, to not be seen as too happy, if we sense our joy makes others feel uncomfortable, or less-than. Be you at all times, rather than acquiescing to the unconscious projections or demands of others. Believe as often as you can that **there is no problem**, just more of your greatness and lightness to discover.

Sometimes, when we have worked so hard on ourselves, we evolve and change in ways we hadn't anticipated. It is like a veil is lifted from our eyes, allowing us to see life differently. This may mean that how we view those with whom we associate can also change, bringing its own set of new challenges and adjustments. During these transformation stages, we can enter a state that is so foreign (and so important for our growth and up-levelling) that we seek to identify a problem, or even manifest one when there isn't one, as we are unconsciously resisting our emergence into greater potential. Part of us wants to slow down the process. We've changed so much or shifted so much that we feel somewhat strange and almost uncomfortable. Finding a 'problem' gives us an excuse to go back to old ways.

Higher states of consciousness may arrive when we've embraced a considerable amount of healing self-care and worked hard to get out from under our stuff. We've released limiting beliefs and patterns to such a degree that we no longer 'feel' like us. We may decide something within us isn't quite right because the newer version of us feels unfamiliar—or perhaps people are responding to us differently. The highs and lows of a stress-infused life drop away, and nothing appears to be 'happening' to engage our attention.

This stage can feel foreign and somewhat flat. What is often occurring during this experience is a transition stage, a place between worlds where we are moving away from the old version of ourselves and into more peace, power and potential. It can be perceived as a 'nothing doing, non-exciting' phase, as our body isn't producing the cortisol and adrenaline that we may have become dependent on. Suddenly, our minds are calmer, and our lives are quieter. If we don't stay aware, we can perceive this new state as lack of motivation or passion, or even misidentify it as boredom.

These stages are beautiful and need to be acknowledged and celebrated rather than negated simply because we haven't quite become accustomed to the current version of us. Often, we've climbed a mountain and are being given a reprieve to stand still and appreciate the view. In this place, we can reflect on how far we've come and where we are yet to go. **There is no problem, only more awareness and more unfolding of you and your potential to come.**

Be grateful for the quieter non-action times, because they are essential for our growth and up-levelling. We can't always be in creative, expansive mode. Seeds, when planted, require nourishment and time to grow and the right season to bloom—as do we. Caring for and loving ourselves requires the same level of acceptance and patience.

Sometimes we need to go within to reflect, to restore and even hibernate while we integrate the new learning and changes that are occurring for us spiritually, emotionally, mentally and even physically. The critical thing is to not seek wrongness in the transition phases. We may not quite be where we want to be yet. We may not be feeling how we want to feel, or even seeing the results of our efforts in the material world, but we can take stock and appreciate what we've left behind and how we've grown, and eagerly anticipate what is to come.

Key questions for me during times when I've decided I'm not feeling how I think I should be feeling are:

- What's right about this I'm not getting?
- What's right about me I'm not getting?

Journalling in response to these questions always brings unexpected insights and helps me to embrace each stage of healing and growth.

We need to retrain ourselves to see our greatness and trust in the unfolding of us. We each have a unique, intricately designed path. Many of us on the spiritual evolutionary path can slip into judgement of ourselves (with undercurrents of perceiving we are not being or doing enough) during times when we are not feeling wonderful or vibrantly approaching our days. Life is contrasts and there is a season for everything. A large part of devotion to extreme self-care (that is what is called for during these times) is embracing all the stages we go through and connecting with our inner well of love to truly receive and perceive that all is well. We will get to where we need to be all in good time, for our highest good.

Love means embracing the entirety of the journey and it also means grasping that perhaps when 'nothing is happening', there's a whole lot happening—it just hasn't been revealed within us and for us yet, but it is on its way. We are laying strong foundations.

MESSAGE FOR YOUR LOVE TO BLOOM

Through devotion and commitment to your self-care, expect more love and more of the miracle of you to unfold. Enjoy all the times during your life where you exist between worlds: transitioning from one place to the next. Life and growth are never linear. Ebb and flow, ebb and flow ...

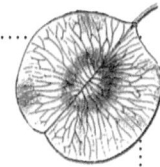

SELF-CARE IDEA FOR TODAY

Respond to perceived problems with questions. Asking questions of our higher selves assists us to gain new perspectives and to access our innate wisdom. Open your journal and write these questions:
- In what ways have I recently up-levelled that I may not have acknowledged?
- How are these changes creating more love within me and my life?

ORACLE CARDS

Oracle cards open windows to wisdom.

Oracle cards are a quintessential aspect of my self-care. They instantly elevate my vibration, increase my presence, and connect me with higher aspects of myself. I feel nurtured and loved when I am communing with oracle and affirmation card decks, as they radiate such positive energy. I am drawn closer to that great, powerful, loving universal force through my oracle card readings.

Oracle cards help us with our day-to-day questions and responses to life. They also assist us to contemplate our deeper 'bigger picture' understanding of the world, our place in it and our divinity.

Oracle cards originally caught my eye in response to my fascination with all elements of the invisible world. It was a means of learning about all the various powerful beings, creatures, gods and goddesses revered around the world and their powerful teachings. Oracle cards helped me to ascertain and appreciate the common elements in many forms of spirituality. They provided me with a method to further enhance my keenly developing intuitive sense. I was also captivated by these beautiful cards as they reminded me of and rekindled my love of swap-card collecting as a child. These tiny little works of art were creatively captured on card and could be viewed one after the other in the palm of my hand. Oracle cards are a source of beauty and creativity.

Oracle cards are great tools for self-care and self-love as they enhance our intuition, our self-awareness, and our connection with the divine. They provide us with positive guidance and elevated vibrations. Just gazing at oracle cards opens the door for intuitive messages to flow to us as we connect with the images and symbols on the cards. They become even more powerful when we ask questions before shuffling our decks and receiving a card.

Some of my favourite questions are:

- What do I need to know today for my highest good?
- What is my next right action for moving forward and evolving?
- If I make this choice, what may show up in my life?

Oracle cards help tune us into the unseen world ... a world that conveys information to us continuously if we are open to receiving it. They help us to develop and utilise our intuition to navigate the world via messages from universal intelligence.

Our intuition is often connected with all that is unspoken or unseen. It is associated with vibes, gut feelings and random thoughts. Initially, these subtle perceptions may not make any sense, particularly if our ego or analytical mind tries to jump in and push them aside. They will, however, have a sense of truth surrounding them that reads strongly for us. The challenge is to keep the intellect and ego mind at bay long enough to hear the whispers that come through for us, often in unexpected moments. These intuitive flashes are how the Universe speaks to us. It is a loving act towards self to learn how to hear them.

Oracle card decks help us to connect with signs and symbols, and before long we start to notice and pay attention to them in our daily living. The cards assist us to stay in alignment with the ebbs and flows of the Universe: as we notice, observe and connect, meaningful coincidences and synchronistic moments become more common. Oracle cards open us to connection with our higher self and to life-changing moments, revelations, light-bulb clarity, and awakening deep wisdom.

I find that different card decks call to me on different days. I know that as they become a part of your life, this will happen for you too. They become non-judgemental 'friends' and guides, always keeping a line of communication open. They are an expert tool for making intuition central to our existence.

When working with the cards, you may hear things and feel things, and receive images, instant knowing and a heightened sense of what is going on around you and within you. Self-knowledge and self-awareness are essential aspects of self-care and self-love. We learn to trust ourselves, which buoys our self-confidence and enhances our self-love.

When doing card readings, we all have unique ways of perceiving which card is calling to us. For me, when I am shuffling a deck and the card arrives that I am meant to pull, there is a sudden change in energy, a lift, an increase in vibration. I feel it in my heart, solar plexus and sacral chakra areas. There's a sense that I need to stop, listen and receive. It is a complex, subtle arising, and as with any skill, we get better with trust in our hearts, confidence in our abilities and lots of practice. It's not something we can control; it is about surrender, receptivity, and receiving in new ways.

Before card readings, I always clear decks of any stored energy, breathe deeply, centre, ground, meditate for a few minutes, surround myself in white light and ask to connect with my divine guidance. It is important to be calm, clear and peaceful before a card reading. Avoid attempting a card reading if you are stressed, emotional or strongly vested in outcomes, as this will scramble the messages and impact their effectiveness.

Stay open to the messages and cards that come through. Sit with the card for a few moments and connect with the images, symbols and descriptors. It is a great idea to use oracle cards as journalling prompts, as they can help us to tune out our minds and connect with the messages coming through for us. Intuitive insights will often begin to come through even before you read the written message.

Sometimes, we may feel a little 'reactive' to a message that comes through, and the musings of the ego may stir. It may not be what we want to hear at this time. Remember (as we learned in *Pearls of Wisdom: For Your Path to Peace*) our reactions, our triggers, are often our best teachers. There is great learning to be had about ourselves via our reactions. Sit with the information, breathe and ask, 'What can I perceive and receive here that I've previously been unwilling or unable to perceive or receive?' This approach will set you free as you will learn to look within and connect with your own innate and powerful wisdom. What a gift to you and your life.

Activate your oracle abilities—they are waiting.

MESSAGE FOR YOUR PATH TO LOVE

As we tune into the energy and healing capacity of the cards, we learn to accept the present moment, clear away emotional clutter, and thus step further into our power. You will discover a deep love and respect for yourself and your intent to awaken. Connect with your innate wisdom and intuition to fully care for you.

Oracle cards give us greater understanding of what is going on within ourselves. They provide increased clarity around what is occurring (for us) in our lives. Self-awareness enhances self-worth, in turn opening us to greater self-love. We feel good when we know what's going on—we feel empowered.

Oracle cards help to clear our minds so we are able to receive information that is helpful rather than a hindrance to our wellbeing and choices. Allow oracle cards to become your own North Star and a divine compass leading you to where you need to go.

SELF-CARE IDEA FOR TODAY

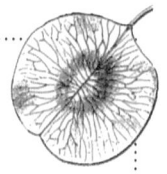

Start to develop your oracle skills by using this book as an oracle. Ask, 'What do I need to know for my highest good in moving forward today?' Next, flick through the pages and stop when you feel called to do so—or simply open the book and see where you land. Read the page and take note of any light-bulb moments, shivers, or emotional responses as you read. These types of reactions often contain the message we require.

OUTSIDE LOOKING IN

Your awareness is a gift to you and the world.

The journey of a leader or a visionary—that is, someone who has a different view of the world and how they would like it to be, or someone choosing a path that is unlike the vocal majority—can be an experience of contrasts. The path of a leader can be one of both inspiration and loneliness.

We have a choice as to whether we take the path of love or fear. Love will allow us to lead, while fear will encourage us to contract and find problems in what we are seeking and creating.

We need to bestow compassion on ourselves when we experience temporary feelings of isolation. This passes quickly when we remember to connect with our higher selves, our super selves. We are never truly alone and are always surrounded by the universal energies and guides helping us to co-create our life.

We can sometimes feel like we are outside the world, perceiving it from a different place and never really fitting in. This is because, on a soul level, we did not come here to fit in: we were born to stand out, to challenge paradigms and to awaken those around us to their potential for light, love, power, peace and wisdom. We signed up for this; we have divine, beautiful, spectacular assignments. This path is not easy and (gratefully) never mundane. We have answered our calling and seek to create a better world. Through answering this call, we discover our own potential for love and all its beautiful derivatives—abundance, joy, adventure, freedom, compassion, forgiveness, success, and divine inspiration—in all that we do and experience.

At times, we may feel like we landed on Earth in the wrong place and at the wrong time without our crew, our tribe. There are no mistakes; we are exactly where we need to be, doing the work we are meant to be doing. Our path along this life to be most effective and most joy infused requires extreme self-care. Our own cups must be full to the brim and overflowing for us to access our greatest potential and serve in the best possible way for ourselves and others.

Through our self-care, we have less chance of being limited, or compromising our health through overwhelm, stress or even from a grief connected with feeling like we are alone without our tribe. We are never alone; our spiritual guidance and support team is always available. Perhaps our 'crew members' are off doing the work they have been chosen to do on this planet and we will meet someday to celebrate great success. We will look back on our lifetime with such a sense of pride, peace and accomplishment—something we may not have achieved unless we had been willing to rise to the challenge of being outside and looking in.

MESSAGE FOR YOUR PATH TO LOVE

Embrace your individuality. Be willing to go where others are not going. You will love you even more when you take risks and rise to the occasions life is asking you to show up for. Your big love will invoke big living.

SELF-CARE IDEA FOR TODAY

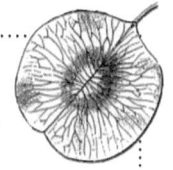

Step outside of your daily existence and ask to be shown the bigger picture, a bird's eye view of your current situation. Ask, 'What am I being called to do or be?' Take out your journal and allow automatic writing to flow from your higher wisdom and guidance team.

PAST LOVES
Love is timeless and transforming.

For many of us, when relationships end, love ends. I guess this is all part of the letting go, the creating space for new love to enter, the releasing of energetic ties, the emerging of a new and wiser self. But what if the love could endure beyond the end of a relationship—even the tumultuous ones—in a different form?

There is much to be learned about ourselves and life through all our relationships, both pleasant and unpleasant. Nurturing self-care is required to successfully navigate our way through ending relationships and ensure we function as the best version of ourselves. If there are children involved, they require the very best of us.

When relationships are breaking down, our worth can be challenged. To limit this possible affront to our self-love, the best approach is to connect with our heart wisdom by directing questions within. *What did I learn about myself through this relationship? What can I learn about love to take into my next relationship? How can I base this transition on love? What forgiveness do I need to invoke to release negative energetic binds?*

It is great to be able to look back and reflect on what was gained from the relationship. Even if the relationship was toxic and tumultuous, we can learn about and identify what it is that we never want to experience again. We have survived, we have shown great strength and we have overcome the parts of ourselves that allowed us to choose non-nurturing and non-expansive relationships.

When time has given us the necessary distance from any pain and loss and gently encouraged us to heal the wounds, let go and move on. Seek forgiveness as your 'go-to' to set yourself free of any toxic energetic ties from the past. Then take it a step further and focus on the love that you originally felt. Allow it to infuse every cell of your being. Use it as fuel to fire feelings of love and heal your body. Keep it impersonal if that works—that is, remember the love without reconnecting with the past relationship or the person. Use these feelings to remind you of the being of love you always were and still are.

Love is unlimited and there is so much more available for you to be and experience. The more love you generate within, the more will be reflected through the eyes of another. From this space, the depth of love that you can receive will be exponentialized. Some love is so strong that it endures throughout time—even when you are no longer with a past love. Allow this love to be what it is without judgement and to bloom within you whenever you choose.

MESSAGE FOR YOUR LOVE TO EVOLVE

Embrace the power of all forms of love, past, present and future—they can all exist simultaneously and very powerfully. What if you kept the love within you that you have felt for every person on your journey through life? How powerful would you be and imagine what you could create from this space! Approaching love in this way is true self-care.

SELF-CARE IDEA FOR TODAY

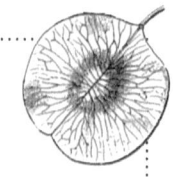

Send love and light to those from your past who you are struggling to forgive. This approach does not condone behaviour or imply that you ever need to see or communicate with them again. What it does is free you of any toxic, limiting binds that you have established with another.

PERFUME

A little dab of perfume is a little splash of self-care.

Scent captivates our senses and elevates our mood. Perfume can turn our feelings from ordinary to extraordinary in a heartbeat. Perfume is love in a bottle: we can feel so good just from the simple act of selecting the right scent for an occasion. The ritual of removing the jewel-like lid and applying it or even enveloping ourselves in it (depending on our individual style of application) is such a joy. Perfume is beauty on display.

Going into a perfumery is a journey into self-care. We are there for the sole purpose of indulgence and decadence. We adoringly gaze at all the spectacularly and lovingly designed bottles and we know we are taking home a little piece of heaven with us. We test various scents until we find one that stirs something within—the one that lights us up and connects us with love. We place it in our handbag and know we are carrying a little splurge of love. We can take this little expression of love out at any time and treat ourselves with a spray of nurturing.

Scent nourishes our senses and our soul. If we aren't perfume wearers, we can still indulge in the power of scent through luxurious bath oils and body creams. Our bodies love to be pampered. As we care for our bodies in this way, they feel so good that they cannot help but infuse love into every cell: heart, body and mind. Whenever I am given the gift of perfume, I know my face says it all: the eyes sparkle, the smile broadens and the heart is warmed—love in action.

My perfume collection feels like an extension of me—each

has been lovingly selected. Each time I gaze upon the beautifully designed and crafted bottles, I smile and am filled with gratitude. I place them lovingly in my room and feel such contentment every time I select one for the day, polish a gorgeous bottle or simply remove the lid for a little treat of scent.

Just as I love words, I am also enamoured by all the magical names specifically chosen for perfumes. How can one not feel good when spraying oneself with a fragrance gifted with the name Terre de Lumiere (which means light of the earth) or Amor Amor (meaning love) or Volupté, meaning intense pleasure that is blissful, sensuous and spiritual. And then there's Princess—all women deserve to feel like a princess, as we are the embodiment of the divine feminine.

Many of my favourite colognes and perfumes have journeyed with me in life through sadness and joy, each having their own unique gifts for healing inner hurt, replenishing my energy, and elevating my mood. Many contain beautiful memories and evoke feelings associated with special events like my wedding day, or specific moments in time to cherish.

MESSAGE FOR YOUR LOVE TO FLOURISH

Connect with your love by gifting to yourself, indulgently. If not you, then who?

SELF-CARE IDEA FOR TODAY

Take a little adventure into a perfumery and see which scent calls to your heart and wants to come live with and nurture you. Perfume is love magic in a bottle—in fact, little genies in a bottle.

PETS

The loving way we talk to our pets should be the way we talk to ourselves.

Pets are invitations to give and receive love. The unconditional love they invoke within us and have for us is highly therapeutic and healing, and therefore gifts us with a deep form of self-care.

Research indicates that our connections with pets have numerous health benefits, including reduction in anxiety, depression, and trauma responses. Having a pet to live with infuses us with love and redirects attention from overthinking our own perceived problems and conditions, towards the needs of our pets.

Our animals invite the best of us to come forward. Pets encourage stillness within. We feel present as they are so present with us.

Just thinking of my West Highland white terriers is enough to warm my heart: simple, yet powerful self-care and opening to love. Our Westies remind me of white, fluffy teddy bears, returning me to childlike feelings of snuggling and feeling safe with my own array of much-loved, precious soft toys.

Caring for and loving our beautiful pets heals us because we function from nurturing elevated emotions through extending our love. The act of giving love nourishes the soul. Anything that lights up the soul is self-care.

My daughter, Julia, has a divine connection with animals. Her pets have always been cherished companions. They appear to be in heaven in her presence; it would not matter what they were doing together. Unconditional love, total presence and an appreciation of each moment are synonymous with what I am lucky enough to witness when I observe Julia with her animals.

I asked Julia what having pets has gifted to her in life:

> Having an animal in your life is like having a little soulmate or best friend. It's an energy and connection that flows between you and your pet. Our pets can't 'speak' to us, yet they are always communicating with us in a way we learn to understand through their unique personalities.
>
> No matter what, your four-legged (or any-legged) friend will always be there for you. If you're needing comfort, someone to talk to, a shoulder to cry on, someone to go on adventures with, or an unconditional listener, they will be there with you in every moment, because you are their world.
>
> All my tears have been cried with Zoe (my West Highland white terrier) on the pillow next to me. She has been my life companion and with me through all the decades I have grown and changed. She has been pushed around in dolls' prams and had tea parties on picnic rugs, and now she has been there for my engagement and moving into my own home. We have shared much love, fun and adventure in our sixteen years together.

When riding her horse, Julia would talk of a connection that she found hard to describe.

> It is a deep respect and love and a sense of oneness, being in tune with one another, almost operating in sync. You put your trust in an animal that is a lot bigger and

stronger than you, yet they are willing to listen to you and respect you if you respect them.

When riding a horse, you share a magical connection that goes beyond just riding them around and telling them what to do. You end up being able to read each other's emotions and communicate through energy. It feels somewhat magical.

MESSAGE FOR YOUR PATH TO LOVE

We heal and flourish as we gift and receive love via our beautiful bonds with pets. Owning a pet is a great responsibility. Spend time around the pets of another if your life circumstances aren't conducive to having one of your own.

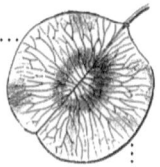

SELF-CARE IDEA FOR TODAY

I find myself really tuning into and listening to how I talk to my puppy—all the cajoling, all the beautiful words indicating how wonderful she is and the extreme declarations of love. Just for today, speak to yourself with the energy and words you would use to talk to an adored pet. Beautiful words are beautiful self-care.

PLAY

Play encourages zest: vigorous and enthusiastic enjoyment of life.

In our adult lives, responsibility, hard work, focus and dedication can reap wonderful rewards. However, to balance our busy 'adult' approach to life, a form of self-care that our inner spirit requires most is play and playfulness. It lightens our mood, brightens our energy, and brings renewed enthusiasm for who we are and what we are doing. Lighten up (through childlike play) to heighten those elevating emotions.

When was the last time you gave yourself permission to be a real silly-billy? Silly Billy is not concerned with what others think of them. They know that the doorway to true contentment opens when we are willing to be ourselves in totality and express this individuality in our own unique ways.

We become too guarded and too constrained within a cage of our own making by allowing ourselves to be 'managed' according to our concern for the judgements of others. We place ourselves in a box and often close the lid when we concede to being defined by the expectations and projections of others. To embrace our Silly Billy, we need to connect back with our inner child, that little person who just wanted to play from moment to moment, who followed joy wherever and whenever possible. They didn't have time to worry about the to-do list or get too serious about all the responsibilities and tasks calling. They were truly present, seeking joy and being playful at every turn. Our childlike self was authentic and vulnerable enough to be who we are, thus enhancing our connections with others, as we were without defensive walls.

There is much healing and peace available to us through remembering our inner child and honouring that place within us that is light and free and seeks opportunities for pleasure, reward, wonder and awe.

As my children were growing, I loved watching them play: the creativity, the excitement, the inventiveness, the power of every blissful moment. It was such a reminder to just lighten up and leave the mountain of responsibilities (of my own making) to themselves for a precious part of every day.

I remember Julia entertaining herself for hours with a cassette, wrapping the tape around the entirety of the house perimeter. On another occasion, she helped herself to the rubber gloves under the sink, filled them with water, drew faces on them and turned them into a 'family', amusing herself for hours. One time, I left Nic 'unsupervised' in the backyard for too long and he dug a pond in the garden, lined it and filled it with water to put fish in it. Another time, he rigged up a flying fox and made a train track out of garden sleepers—very industrious and creative! Julia and I would be entertained for days after Nic had watched a much-loved movie, as he would very creatively re-enact many of the scenes.

Many of us reserve play for holidays. If we could incorporate play into every day, our spirits would experience an inner 'holiday spirit' and our stress levels would most certainly decrease. Asking the questions *What would my inner child like me to know today?* and *How would my inner child like me to play today?* opened me to a new dimension of self-care through understanding the essential nature of play.

What would my inner child like me to know today?

- Relax more into the flow of life
- Ease your pace

- Do less to attract more
- Be kinder
- Be more nurturing
- Laugh lots
- Be silly, playful and frivolous
- Remember how mischievous you are and be it
- All is well, you've got this and there's plenty of time for play

How would my inner child like me to play today?

- Take the time to see the funny side of everything.
- Be light, merry and playful, and model this for the people you encounter today. It will be contagiously wonderful.

The contentment and honouring of deeply held and often forgotten desires (that were revealed through the play I loved as a child) also enhanced the love flowing within me and through my life. I found that my 'adult responsibilities' became beautifully dipped in elements of frivolity—I learned to lighten up in all areas of life. I could bring my childhood 'Christmas Day feeling' into all that I did—it was a choice, and I was determined to choose it often.

Living through our inner child is living through our heart, our love. We remember and connect back to our true essence. There is also much wisdom to be gained, as our childhood 'lives' hold significant keys to helping us understand what we would truly love to be doing in our adult lives—providing clues to possible career choices that would light us up from within.

Observe a child to connect with the healing power of play!
There is one little girl that comes to mind who inspires me and captivates me with her play. This little lady plays from moment to

moment, filling every second with bliss, creativity and excitement. One minute, she is pretending to be a hairdresser and putting silver aluminium paper in her hair as foils, next she is applying make-up with her play make-up kit, then she is bathing her Barbies in the kitchen sink in bubble bath. There is not a moment to waste in this whirlwind of play and creative genius. Then, it's on to making a cubbyhouse with the lounge room furniture and every blanket and towel in sight. Now, it's time for grooming her (rocking) horse, complete with brushes and a hairdresser's spray bottle. The possibilities, ideas and imagination are simply infinite! What a way to live!

Reconnect with childhood memories to reactivate your sense of play. On a recent island holiday where the only form of transport allowed is golf buggies, I had all these beautiful memories of how much I loved Enid Blyton's Noddy stories. The buggies reminded me of his toy car, and I was immediately taken back in time to the vibe of childhood—such is the power of beautiful memories. I couldn't wait to find one of these books and reconnect with the magic.

MESSAGE FOR YOUR PATH TO LOVE

> Play leads to inspiration. We all require more inspiration in our lives to navigate tempestuous times.
> Play like there's no tomorrow. Play will heal you, release you and set you free to be more of you.

SELF-CARE IDEA FOR TODAY

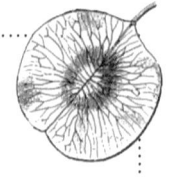

Lightness and brightness for our souls is beautiful self-care. Embrace the enthusiasm, wonder, awe and curiosity that led you as a child to live your best life. Close your eyes and transport yourself back to the most idyllic times in your childhood. What can you see? What are you loving? What might you like to revisit today?

POETRY AND WORDS

Words are powerful—uplifting, inspiring, nurturing, caressing, inviting, healing and encouraging.

Words move us, guide us and challenge us. Learning to ask questions with our wise words opens us to the power and benevolence of the Universe. Words can create healing movements. We are changed through conversations, stories and writing. The power of truly being present with another and deeply listening cannot be underestimated. Harmonious communication is such a gift for us and others. Great quotes inspire us to look within and gain fresh wisdom and points of view.

Tune into the power and potential of words to invoke inner change and fresh ways of perceiving and receiving. I am a wordsmith. I spin words to heal and transform myself and others. How can you use words powerfully to create change within yourself and others?

Perhaps one of the most beautiful combinations of words is presented in the form of poetry. Poetry teaches us to look deeper; there is always more below the surface to be revealed. Poets are true wordsmiths. As a writer, the literary techniques, the imagery, the metaphors, the personification quite simply light me up. Anything that lights us up is self-care and an expression of love.

Poetry has a language of its own: expertly combining words, colour, concepts, sounds, rhythm, feelings, thoughts and symbols that invoke a uniquely personal response in a reader. Poems have a unique way of both concealing and revealing, awakening us to our own complex intelligence.

Beautiful poetry speaks to us in the language of love. Poems soothe and uplift us. They allow us to connect with and reveal deep emotions and wisdom.

Poetry provides a doorway to the sacred within us, to knowledge that may have been previously obscured from us. A powerful poem has the potential to awaken us to aspects of ourselves and to new thinking that may have been previously closed to us.

Poetry is very mysterious and spiritual, cloaked in deep layers of meaning.

Through poetry, we can work with themes that are deeply personal to us. There are poems to immerse us in beauty, in love, in healing, in nature, in inspiration. There is a poem for understanding and connecting with every element of the human condition. Poetry helps us to unlock our innate intelligence. When engaging with an expertly crafted poem, we seek to receive information often coded very deeply within the nuances and themes involved.

A poet shares their unique experiences and interpretations of the world with us, and in so doing asks us to reflect and develop our own understanding.

Poetry is pure presence. To connect with the meaning of a poem, we need to be still and quiet enough to receive the messages and themes. Anything in our busy world that allows us to be present, still and calm is a loving act of self-care.

Poetry is highly nourishing soul food. It instils deep reverence, respect, gratitude and appreciation of the complexity of and unique responses to (and interpretations of) life. Poetry brings colour, hope, awe and wonder into our being on days when these may be waning.

Poems enhance our cognitive function. Understanding and learning new words makes us feel good about ourselves and helps us to articulate our feelings and express ourselves more effectively.

If you feel moved to create poetry, you are gifting yourself and the world with the healing power of words. Your creations have the potential to create greater self-awareness, as poetry encourages us to go within to seek meaning.

Your poems could help heal emotional wounds. They could provide knowledge and inspiration for others and encourage the celebration of life. Your poems have the power to create awe and wonder for the myriad of experiences of life.

Poetry is therapy. It helps us to understand ourselves and others and to process experiences and change our perceptions. Poetry opens us to new ways of being, perceiving, receiving, and responding to life. It can help us to better understand our own mind and therefore alleviate anxiety and depression. The experiences of others that are revealed in poems shed light on our understanding of self.

MESSAGE FOR YOUR LOVE TO BLOOM

Carry a poem in your pocket. Feel and be the passion, wisdom, mystery, beauty and inspiration that the poet infused into their creative work. Many poems have the power of love flowing through them—someone has taken the time to form some powerful words to serve and to make a difference.

Learn to love words, for they are a spark that connects you to the love within you and for all of life.

'Poetry lifts the veil from the hidden beauty of the world ...'
— Percy Bysshe Shelley

SELF-CARE IDEA FOR TODAY

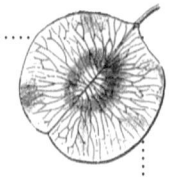

Read some poetry. Share the gift and beauty of poetry with a friend, or perhaps the world. Imagine how special an individual would feel to receive a poem crafted or selected just for them: love in action.

We don't need to be poets to write poetry. Just let some words flow, as in my poem for you:

Your Seeds

Your seeds are within you, awaiting you
Your love is ready to flourish
Nourish, nurture and water
Emerge into the sun
The world needs your radiance
You are in bloom
Unfurl some more

POINTS OF VIEW

*Our points of view are the lenses through
which we see, perceive, receive
and experience the world.*

Our points of view, over time, have a monumental impact on our wellbeing and life in general. They shape us, define us and determine what we allow into our world. Our beliefs fashion what we perceive, receive and conversely what we block from flowing into our lives. If part of us believes we aren't really deserving of what we desire to call in, then on some level, even if unconscious, we will engage in self-sabotage. Our ability to care for ourselves and love ourselves is greatly influenced by how we believe life works, the value we place on ourselves, and the role we play in the grander web weaving of our life. Our points of view become our default system, our underpinning core, influencing our choices and actions.

Our task is to become aware of our points of view, particularly those we may have adopted from family members at a young age. Much unlearning is often required of old thinking before we can establish newer, more life-enhancing points of view. Some points of view are so ingrained that they can be automatic and unrecognised for some time. Even those that are deep can be uncovered and reworked to better suit the life that we would like to create—and at the same time represent how we would truly like to be and feel. We have the choice; we are that powerful. Shining love on outdated, limiting points of view can transform them into something that serves as a catalyst for our greatest potential. We uncover limiting points of view with deep care and deep presence, which strengthen our connection with the transmuting potential of our inner well of love.

Examining our points of view can be most enlightening when intending to enhance our ability to receive and be love. They can help define the way we wish to be, how we choose to feel and how we would like to show up in life.

When they are uplifting, our points of view can bring such peace and love to our lives. Our points of view can care for us or limit us. They have the power to change our energy and our energy has the power to change our life. Examine yours today.

Some points of view that I have encouraged myself to embrace for defining me and my reality and sustaining my state of love are:

- I love life and it loves me right back.
- I find joy in all that I do and all that I am.
- I am a receptacle for great receiving.
- I use my power first and foremost for me and then for others.
- I follow my own divinely guided path to freedom.
- My power is for serving me and the world and knows no bounds. I am free.
- The right relationships, just perfect for me, always find me.
- My children are blessed on this earth.
- No one is more powerful than me.
- No one and no thing can bring me down.
- My energy is one hundred per cent my own.
- My energy is protected at all times.
- Things happen for me in divine timing.
- Love and miracles surround me.
- My body and life heal me every minute of every day.
- I am always connected to love.
- The beautiful unknown opens with possibilities and adventure.

- My life unfolds as one blissful experience to the next and to the next.
- That is not my circus and not my monkeys.
- It is not my job to take on the suffering of others, but to assist healing and transform suffering into light and love.
- I cannot change what is not mine to change.
- Peace is my barometer, showing me where I am on the scale of love.
- My great work deserves to be shared, loved and appreciated.
- My path is divinely guided and there are no mistakes, just detours in the right direction.
- Abundance is my divine birthright.
- I create and receive miracles of all kinds.
- I am no less and no more than another.
- We are all at unique stages of the journey. I respect each person's passage and place within the grand web of life.
- I can't fail, unless I give up.
- I do the work I came here to do, regardless of motivation issues, resistance or fear.
- I rise, up-level and evolve through all that I do and experience.
- I am on a healing journey until the day I leave this planet.
- I am here to create light, love, awakening, joy, abundance, freedom and transformation.
- I am an expression of love.
- My life is an expression of love.
- I feel love within me and all around me.

MESSAGE FOR YOUR LOVE TO EXPAND

Changing our points of view can allow us to let go of who we thought we were and become who we truly are—both a source and a unique expression of unconditional love. The kind of love that is there just because it's there—an intrinsic, untouchable part of us.

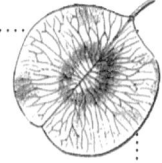

SELF-CARE IDEA FOR TODAY

Live a life where love is the foundation. Write down the points of view that are going to shape your love-filled reality from this day forward.

POWER

*Our power and love emerge day by day
through our self-care.*

Our self-care empowers us. It assists us to take back our power in places where we were disempowered. Our self-care and love make us feel safe enough to trust in ourselves and life again, healing us back to wholeness: where our true power arises.

Power is rising above the conditioning, the limitations and the thoughts, feelings, emotions, projections and expectations of others, and at the same time connecting deeply with our own worth and love, shining it and being it in all its glory, authenticity and magic. Your power is a divine force for change and awakening.

> 'True power is gentle, not forceful.'
> — Alan Cohen

Power resides within all of us. It is our divine birthright and can only be accessed in its purest, most effective form through love. Power that is born through the ego will not be of great service to ourselves and the world. It will make demands and even lead to harmful choices and actions. Power that arises through love creates movement, magic, infinite possibilities and miracles, as it flows through us from our higher selves and divine connection. This kind of power (when it arises within) calls us to step up, to lead and to be the greatest version of ourselves to best serve ourselves and the worlds we inhabit. Authentic power is about being the invitation for others to step more into their own power: to choose to be more, receive more.

Our power is tied to our ability to receive, to access life and to create abundant living. If we don't access our own power, we too freely give it away to others or to those we perceive have authority.

Our arising power requires that we no longer shrink or play small to make others feel more comfortable around us; this harms us as we try to squeeze ourselves into tiny, uncomfortable, stifling boxes. We don't create movements, change or inspiration from spaces where we try to contort ourselves to fit in. We need to be our authentic selves, which means standing tall in our power, confidence and presence. It feels amazing to be in this space once we accept it, own it and be it. It just takes practice and the willingness to shine within and outwards.

When we try to limit our power and make ourselves go small, unseen and unheard, we tend to lower our vibration so much that we open ourselves up to feelings of self-doubt, self-judgement and guilt. By attempting to make others feel better around us, we can make ourselves feel awful. This is not self-care, and it is not self-love. It does not elevate the energy and power of those around us—we all stay muted.

Deep within, our spirit is calling us to love and care for ourselves and our wellbeing enough to rise up, to step up, to show up, and energetically encourage others to do the same. Yes, some individuals may be initially uncomfortable in our powerful presence: hopefully our power will create some cracks in the veneer of their perceived powerlessness, encouraging them to sense the power that may be calling to emerge within them.

When we do at last give up resistance and fully accept and embrace our power, it feels amazing, as we connect with our true selves. We are calm and grounded and peaceful as we are not using our power against ourselves. Often, our health improves because all our energy is now used for us rather than against us.

It takes an inordinate amount of energy to divorce who we truly are by subverting our power. It is a loving act to fully receive all that we are. With our power fully activated and supporting us and our lives, we draw in our life purpose, our calling, our path, our mission. We show up for life and it shows up for us in innumerable ways.

Through owning our power and being all that we are meant to be, we are connected to the most powerful force of all: love. Love and the Universe continue to expand and grow, and we need to do this too.

How can you meet your power and integrate it into every cell of your being?
Some possible portals into your power are to:

- Embrace daily unapologetic, extreme self-care.
- Love yourself unconditionally and allow this to express itself often.
- Connect with powerful people and catch yourself before you go to make yourself 'less-than'.
- Creativity is power; be a creative expression of you today.
- Surround yourself with images and symbols that signify rising power: fire, dragons, phoenixes, number combinations, electrical storms, tsunamis (reflecting tsunamis of consciousness) and shooting stars.
- Allow love to radiate throughout every cell in your body and out into the world.
- Embrace Dr Wayne Dyer's approach to life: believe it and you will see it.
- See the beauty within you and all around you. It will build your love of self and others, which is your power in action.
- Exercise: a powerful body creates a powerful mind and energy.

- Breathing and relaxation practices—our peace connects us with our power.
- Patience is power—know you have all the time in the world.
- Know you don't have to be perfect to be powerful—we are all a beautiful work in progress.
- Listen to guidance.
- Learn from your triggers; those reactions that take you away from your power.
- Foster points of view like, *I allow my power to surge and rise*, or *I am a shooting star*, or *My star is rising* to support the emergence of your power.
- Be present and embrace stillness—there is power and potential in our stillness.
- Find passion and purpose: they are doorways to our power.
- Connect with the power of nature: crashing ocean waves, sun streaming into your body and wind blowing away all your cares.
- Put yourself in situations that challenge your power and your willingness to step into it—no more hiding quietly away.
- Socialise—lots of opportunities for practising connecting with our power are available in social situations, as we experience live power plays in action.
- Connect with your inner wisdom and guidance; it knows everything you have put in place to limit your power.
- Read inspirational stories of those who have stepped into their power and are using it to make a positive impact in the world.
- Clear your energy and create strong, protected boundaries.

- Release that which does not belong to you: it is not your job to take on the pain of others, but your power may transmute it.
- Stay in your own lane.
- Have no resistance to what is; just flow.
- Replace control with surrender.
- Love yourself and all that life presents for you, as gratitude builds love and power.
- Know in your heart that you are the only one powerful enough to stop you.
- Listen to power songs like Katy Perry's 'Rise' or Rachel Platten's 'Fight Song'.
- Vulnerability is strength; seek support as you require it or desire it.
- Take control of your mind, only allowing positive thoughts and stories about you to have airplay.
- Watch superhero movies.
- Trust yourself and all of life, as fear steals our power. Be fearless.
- Release worry; it voids our power.
- Meditate and visualise yourself standing in your power and bravery in a myriad of circumstances. It might be speaking in front of an audience; walking into a room, and shining; confidently expressing yourself; successfully taking a risk; or trying something new.
- Befriend crystals and their wisdom and enlightening and healing properties.
- Embrace energy healing and energy medicine to get free of self-sabotage and self-imposed limitations.
- Have deep faith in your path and purpose on this planet. Speak your truth to those who can hear it. Celebrate you and your achievements, no matter how seemingly small—the small ones are often the grandest.

'Everything is within your power and your power is with you.'
— Janice Trachtman

MESSAGE FOR YOUR LOVE TO BLOOM

Divine power is activated when there is enough love within to receive and nurture it. Accessing our power is a loving act of service towards ourselves and others. Being all we can be changes the world.

Adventures abound when you are unbound. Claim your power, shine brightly and embrace 'no more dimming to fit in'. Become the leader of your own life. Allow your nobility and grace to be palpable, to be felt beyond words, through your presence. Step out of the shadows and become a beacon for others. Empower others with your power. You are a leader.

SELF-CARE IDEA FOR TODAY

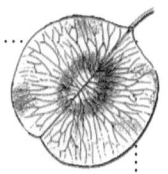

Create journal prompts to help you access your power, perhaps using some of the questions below. Allow the insight to flow.

- How can love connect me with my power in this moment?
- How would love and power act here?
- What power can I embrace and activate now?
- How can my power serve today?
- How can I meet my power and integrate it into every cell of my being?
- What portals into my power are available today?
- What can I release that will allow me to access my power?

Placing your hand on your heart and connecting with love before you ask these questions is a very powerful practice.

RAINBOWS

*Rainbows are doorways to
hopes and dreams.*

The word 'rainbow' influences my very being. Looking at real rainbows or images of them elevates my emotions. I feel blessed. Seeing them span the skies moves my spirit to soar upwards alongside them. I associate rainbows with receiving beyond my current reality and reaching for greater possibilities. They are symbolic of the magic and the wonder of fairytales.

Rainbows are signs of reassurance that all is well; there are reasons for hope and optimism. After the storms in life, brightness and happiness can descend. Rainbows remind me that there are 'pots of gold' waiting for me to discover and receive. They feel like a message from the heavens to remember our beautiful, loving spiritual natures and power.

Rainbows draw me back to my innate creativity when I connect with the magnitude of the colourful display before me. We can witness the depths of creativity that are possible in this universe if we are willing to stop, see, perceive and receive.

The colours of the rainbow remind me of the diversity of life and that a full spectrum of colour creates beautiful light.

Rainbows call us to be present, as there is often very little in the moment that can compete with their spectacular nature and the diverse impact on the soul of the observer.

The chakra system is based on the colours of the rainbow and reminds me of the healing power of colour. Wear yellow to feel more powerful, confident, optimistic and joyful. Dress in orange to spark creativity and adventure, and to encourage feelings of warmth and enthusiasm. Adorn yourself in purple to connect with higher guidance, wisdom, imagination, intuition, magic, emotional balance and the power to transform. Drape yourself in green to heal and promote growth, harmony and abundance. Wear pink to invoke love, affection, grace, kindness, beauty, nurturing and compassion. Surround yourself in white for peace, purity, and cleansing energies and as a reminder to stand in the light. Wear silver to deflect unwanted energies and enhance intuition. Clothe yourself in black to feel strong, independent and protected. Wear red for bravery and for commanding attention, invoking passion and creating seductive moods. Surround yourself in blue to invoke feelings of calm and tranquillity.

Rainbows are a universal symbol of love. They are stunning miracles of nature and an instant connection to wonder and awe. Each time I witness a rainbow, I feel special, as it feels like this stunning display has appeared just for me.

MESSAGE FOR YOUR PATH TO LOVE

Rainbows connect us with love because of the very nature of the qualities they invoke within us: wonder, awe, excitement and being grateful for the blessings that are on the way for us. Look above and observe ... and feel hope for and reassurance of great things to come.

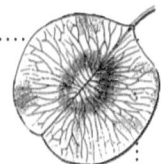

SELF-CARE IDEA FOR TODAY

Take out your sketchbook and colour a rainbow today. As you are creating, drift off ... hope and dream of some new possibilities.

READING AND RESEARCH

Unlock your wisdom through the wisdom of others.

There are truly spectacular people in the world doing beyond amazing things to help us on our travels through life. Tap into their knowledge and expertise to catapult your own wisdom and awakening. We move further away from our human selves and closer to our super selves with each step towards unlocking not only our own wisdom, but the great depth of universal wisdom that is available for us.

Pick up a book that calls to you, or falls into your lap, or appears on your newsfeed, or is recommended to you, or catches your attention from a magazine. These synchronistic occurrences are created just for us, as we are designed for and drawn towards evolving in ways ideal for us. The pathways and guidance available are unique to all of us—such is the magic of the words of wisdom contained within the writings of others.

There is a oneness on this planet. This means that, as one person awakens to new wisdom, so do many others. All those we connect with (in any way) are touched by our unfoldment. Integral teachings and fresh understanding required for our growth are often downloaded onto the planet simultaneously in a myriad of ways. That is why new ideas often appear via many spiritual teachers at once. We are connected to the same source of universal wisdom. Each person represents this wisdom in a unique way, in their unique voice. There is a voice for us all to resonate with somewhere in the world.

Reading is a high-vibrational, presence-inducing experience.

It is a great form of self-care, as we are actively seeking to up-level our self-awareness and therefore our self-worth. What a loving act towards self and to those lucky individuals in our lives, as we then gift them (oftentimes energetically) our newfound awareness. That is enlightening.

MESSAGE FOR YOUR PATH TO LOVE

We are all connected and learn from each other. Open your heart to love by reading the works of those who have developed their knowledge around moving from fear to love. Their paths may make yours clearer.
Many brave souls are pioneers—bringing new thinking onto our planet. Which new thought leaders might you like to embrace?

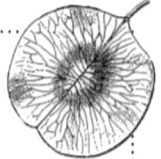

SELF-CARE IDEA FOR TODAY

Browse through the transformational literature section of your local bookshop or library, or favourite online bookseller. Study some titles, covers and blurbs to see what captivates and calls to your unfolding wisdom and love.

RISING THROUGH STORIES

Share your story. Allow your triumphs over adversity to inspire others.

I recently and bizarrely watched two movies (within two days of each other) that had never previously been on my radar. These movies were *I, Tonya*, followed by *Tina*—a film taking an intimate look at the life and career of Tina Turner, carrying on from the singer's 1986 autobiography, *I, Tina*. A synchronistic coincidence designed perfectly for me … I think so. Not to mention that several months before, I had awoken with the Tina Turner song 'Simply the Best' running through my head. I perceive these types of occurrences to be the beginning of many calls and nudges to step up and show up—more than I am currently allowing or willing.

The way Tina survived (and then thrived) through what I judged to be horrendous living conditions, particularly regarding relationships that were the antithesis of love, had the effect of making me seriously consider 'I, Jane' and where Jane was limiting herself. If these women could survive and move towards thriving, whilst rising above their circumstances, then I was inspired to also rise above any perceived limiting trauma in my life.

I think we all have our own versions of trauma, and the power these versions have over us is often exponentialized by the narrative we attribute to such events—the running commentary and emotions that we continue to loop back to, through them. My version of trauma was so minimal in comparison to what others have experienced, but it was still 'my trauma' and I was allowing it to be a background controller in my life.

I believe each of us has some degree of trauma to release before we can move into being the most powerful, creative and influential version of ourselves. My approach became one of no more excuses and no more giving in to self-doubt-inducing personal stories that were impacting my choices or negatively influencing what I could be, perceive and receive in this world.

Recruit help if necessary to craft (or rewrite) and believe the personally scripted stories that are in alignment with you and who you want to be. When you have inner stories that reflect your greater truth, you get to be an expression of those beliefs and live with authenticity. Peace and self-love will be more evident, as you will have greater self-respect.

Our beliefs evolve and change as we awaken. We never reach a place of *I'm all sorted, I'm all done*. We are spectacular, infinite, unlimited works in progress. Adopting the stance of *What else is possible for me and my life?* opens the door for continued up-levelling and for conscious awareness to reveal itself in any given moment throughout our lives. Self-care builds the necessary resilience to continue to grow.

There are a multitude of transformational stories out there to inspire us to be more of ourselves. Oprah Winfrey is another extraordinary 'arisen' woman who comes to mind. Like Tina's story, Oprah's story also challenged me to step up, to show up, to be seen, to be heard and to access more of my potential.

Stories of women overcoming insurmountable odds (to do great things with their lives) put me in a state of *How dare I not step up?* I became committed to getting free of limiting myself by showing up just a little, or just enough. I moved towards being willing to shine far more of my love, light, power and presence. I chose to no longer hide or play small to feel safe. I adopted the approach of: *Okay, Universe, I am here to serve. What do you require of me? Take the reins as I am yours to guide. Where would you have me go? What would you have me do? What would you have me say and to whom? I am one hundred per cent ready, willing and able to back myself and my work and step more fully into my divine mission.*

Inspirational stories were just the push I needed to demand more of myself. Ask the Universe to place in your path the right stories (whether it be through books, movies or speakers) to help you evolve even further along your path. It will feel great to be free.

Being committed to our own freedom and to uncovering our wisdom and the accompanying greatest expression of ourselves is an act of self-love; the love that ripples out around us from this stance is unparalleled.

Movements can start through the sharing of our stories. What story could you share to inspire others to transform their suffering into potential? Liberate yourself and share your own stories if you are moved to do so. Think of the power and momentum that the #MeToo movement continues to make in the lives of women. We are immeasurably powerful when we choose to rise up—particularly together. The words 'warrior women' come to mind. We become unstoppable forces of light and the world so needs this right now.

MESSAGE FOR YOUR PATH TO LOVE

Are you aware of the story that you tell others about who you are? Our story begins in our mind. We teach others how to treat us via the stories we have on repeat about ourselves. How people respond to us is often a mirror reflecting to us our own inner beliefs and truths.

Our stories can begin in our childhood and almost become conditioned responses that define our world, as they represent our beliefs about how life works and our place within it.

If there's anything that you would like to be different in your life, start adjusting the story you tell yourself and others about you. Paint a picture of worthiness and beauty and trust in life, and believe in miracles to create a new story beyond your wildest dreams.

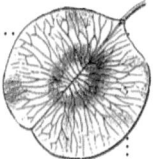

SELF-CARE IDEA FOR TODAY

Which person and their journey from adversity to greatness most inspires you? Read their story as fuel for your own unfolding potential.

SANCTUARY

A beautiful haven is a gift and foundation for our self-care.

In these times of peace, interspersed with times of contrast and chaos combined with our experience of the numerous ways in which dark plays against light in our lives—one of the greatest forms of self-care and a definite ode to love is creating our home as a sanctuary: a haven, a place that nurtures us and lights us up from within.

Having a place to retreat to, a place of restoration and peace to come home to when we have been out and about working our light in the world, is a gift to self. It would be most advantageous if our homes could be filled with beauty: beautiful spaces, gorgeous design elements and things that we like to gaze upon.

The desire to create beautiful spaces is innate within those who seek love. If I look back over all the homes I have ever lived in (even tiny university dorms and less-than-desirable shared student homes) I have always sought to create cosy, beautiful spaces. The great thing is, we can do this anywhere and on any budget. We can start by clearing our space of clutter. If it doesn't hold special significance, is not beautiful to look at, or does not have any practical value … does it really need to be in our sanctuary?

Essential ingredients for my sanctuary are flowers, plants in creative pots, unique pieces of furniture, candles, artwork, prints, colour, beautiful book displays, gorgeous lamps and lighting, and comforting, soft furnishings.

Developing our sanctuary is where our unique expression and divine creativity can come through for us. Create a sacred space in your home just for you. Fill it with items that uplift and inspire you—perhaps beautiful crystals, flowers, candles, uplifting quotes, images, books, shells, feathers, and oracle decks.

Creativity is vital for our health and wellbeing, and home decorating provides our own daily canvas for this to unfold in a beautiful way. Have you noticed how present and uplifted you feel when sourcing, planning and designing home spaces, and how wonderful it feels to open the front door and enter after being away for any length of time?

As well as the physical aspects of our homes, we also need to consider the energy that surrounds us within our spaces. Some of my favourite ways of elevating the energy within a room and clearing energies, are sage smudging, fresh air, adopting some feng shui elements, crystals in strategic locations, sun-facing windows, natural light, some windows open to starlight of a night, salt lamps, floral arrangements, lush plants and energetically blessing spaces upon entry. Having gratitude for everything and everyone in the home also raises the vibration of our sanctuary, along with regular reiki for house members so their energies are elevated and clear, which contributes positively to the overall vibe of the haven.

No matter how beautifully our homes are created, unless great relationships proliferate, the quality of a sanctuary will be compromised. We need to consider the people we allow to share our space, and the expectations we have for behaviour and communication style. What are our boundaries? That is, what do we consider acceptable and unacceptable behaviour, attitudes and practices within our home? Are all members contributing equally in some way to reduce the possibility of resentment arising?

If you are in a home where peace is not evident—where relationships are toxic, and words can be poison—know that you are worth more than this. Take small, daily steps to change home dynamics. If all else fails or repeatedly breaks down despite all your efforts, consider creating a new home for yourself or ask those who are adult enough to take responsibility for themselves to leave. There is never any place for violence in a home no matter how accustomed and 'immune' to it some individuals may become. There is always hope, faith, possibility, intervention, support and love available to generate change. Your life is too precious to have a home that is anything but a sanctuary.

MESSAGE FOR YOUR PATH TO LOVE

Honour yourself by creating a nurturing home environment: one that is beautiful for your senses and nourishing of your emotions.

SELF-CARE IDEA FOR TODAY

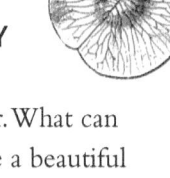

It's time for a sanctuary review and declutter. What can you part with that does not make your home a beautiful place to flourish and bloom in? What can you release to make space for something even better? What can you add to your home that would light you up this day?

SERVICE

Service is a means to express our love.

The love within us always seeks to serve. When we serve and care for others, we are also serving and caring for ourselves. Giving and receiving, when in balance, are reciprocal acts. The magical thing is that when we serve, Universe always responds likewise and seeks to serve us.

Serving sets blessings in motion for the giver and the recipient of love. Open your heart to yourself as much as you do others to find your love. The Universe celebrates when we bestow gifts upon ourselves. Conjure for yourself as much goodness as you can imagine. Be a magician through your service to self and others, in equal measure.

Serving does not always need to involve deeds. Serving can be a quiet, almost impersonal overture of love. Our presence and love serve others by empowering and supporting them.

When we extend kindness to others, they are uplifted, and so are we. As we elevate another in any way, we raise our own vibration and connection to love.

Being in service can be as simple as smiling at a stranger, holding a door open for someone or giving a heartfelt compliment. The power of compliments can never be underestimated—providing little sparks of light and joy for the giver and the receiver.

Adding to the life and wellbeing of another creates abundance of much of what is good in life, for us all. Generosity of spirit is love in action. The innate wisdom we all possess regarding the benefits of serving is so powerful that, if we do not serve others (when we know this is required of us), we will feel moments of unease.

In life, there are times when we don't feel good and do not have the energy or inclination to assist others. Effective service is about timing, intuition and motivation. True service is about quality, not quantity. We may be dealing with personal things that require all our energy and resources. This is okay; we cannot serve all the time and nor is this required of us. Oftentimes, our souls demand that we serve ourselves with our self-care. What do we do when service is not on our agenda? We care for ourselves to the point that we have enough love and energy within to gift it to others when we are moved to do so.

Many of us have been conditioned to believe that we should put ourselves last and save others first, perhaps as the only way to feel good, or to boost our fragile self-worth. The opposite is true. We are of great service when we heal ourselves and take care of ourselves first. Anything less than our best selves contributing to others depletes us and is somewhat ineffective. Gifting care from a place of exhaustion is often tinged with resentment as we wonder, when is it our turn for support?

Our own self-care provides the fortified foundations for anything else to be built upon. We need to care for ourselves like we are the chosen ones here to change the world. Taking care only of others gives us the excuse of never having to look within to get free of our own limiting beliefs and patterns, as we are too busy for that.

As I have evolved, I have learned to not be quite so selective with my service, regarding who and where I flow my energy to. Initially, there was an element of judgement involved. My service was often given according to who I liked or deemed worthy, and delivered to those who didn't annoy me, and perhaps withdrawn from those I'd judged had too much already. We do separation (and that's the opposite of what we want to be doing) when we withhold love from those who don't look like us, act like us or have similar belief systems to us.

Teaching was great training for getting over selective giving, as in a class of twenty-eight, the children, regardless of their 'qualities', all had to be treated and given to equally. I will admit I found this easier as I was paid to do this; it was my job, my career. The challenge came with acquaintances, family and friends who I had put in the aforementioned less-deserving categories.

When it comes to how I may at times have withheld service according to judgements around deservedness, Caroline Myss says that we should get over the fear of empowering others, as a rising tide lifts all ships. Every time we move from resenting others (who we perceive have what we desire) to holding a space of joy for them, we move closer to love.

Ask for divine assistance to serve effectively (without judgement) and to speak and think towards others in positive ways. Even thinking about another person negatively or positively impacts our own vibration and wellbeing. Hijacking another's joy through subtle put-downs or promoting doubt is the opposite of caring for ourselves, as we will not feel good. Being kind to others cares for you. Helping others does not mean something is being taken away from us; quite the opposite is true. Tolerance and patience help us to serve when serving is not something we momentarily wish to do—here, effective service could be as simple as just saying to ourselves, *Bless them*, or *Forgive them, for they know not what they do*. Anything is better than judgement or separation when we are trying to serve from a place of love.

The ways we serve change throughout our lifetime. As we change, up-level and step further into our wisdom and potential, we will be drawn to new ways of serving. We will draw to us the types of service that are most in alignment with us: facilitating the best use of our talents and abilities for the highest good of all.

Service, for me, began in my teenage years when I was working in fashion boutiques and helping to select gorgeous outfits for clients to make them feel beautiful. Having children and being a mother was an incredible service assignment. Sometimes, that may be all the service that is required of us, especially if we have children with special needs. Step-parenting is also a form of service requiring us to stretch our potential in new ways, embracing tolerance and compassion. Service hit a new level during the decades of my teaching career. Next, service presented itself in the form of my energy healing, intuitive counselling and life-coaching business. Now, on a larger scale, writing has become a way of contributing and serving—first through my Facebook posts (Reiki One Jane Holman) and then through books. My books are of service to self and others and are an act of creative love.

Service moves us from our smaller selves into our super selves, based on love. Through service, we can set the meanderings of our mind (that may be at times consumed by less-than-positive thoughts) aside and flow with grace. When serving, we elevate our vibration, as we are contributing to the whole. Our actions (although they may seem minor) raise the collective vibration, because we are all connected.

Be aware of over-giving, and of times when you might be over-caring for others to ease your own feelings of unworthiness, or to distract yourself from the inner work that may be calling for you to address. Over-giving can become addictive, numbing us to our own needs. When we over-give, it can lead to stress and ill health.

Over-giving is the opposite of self-care. To be most effective in our service, our first duty is to care for ourselves. We fill up our own cup as our priority, enabling us to function from our empowered selves when serving. From here, our service will also fuel us, helping us to feel lighter, brighter and in tune with the cosmic field of love.

Our service has ripple effects, and we never know just how far-reaching and dynamic it will be for others. Hope and care infused within others is life enhancing and life changing. That is the magic. Gift some of your magic today; you have it within you more than you know. Isn't it time you released it—especially if it is part of your mission and purpose this lifetime?

MESSAGE FOR YOUR LOVE TO BLOOM

Acts of service lift others by making them feel valued, seen and supported—and at the same time raise our own vibration. Giving and receiving is an art of balance and intuition: knowing when each is most required and best given (and in what form) for maximum impact.

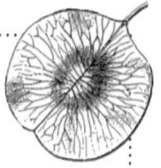

SELF-CARE IDEA FOR TODAY

Ask: *Dear Universe/God/guides/angels*
(whatever it is for you):

- How may I serve?
- What would you like me to do?
- Where would you like me to go?
- What would you have me say and to whom?

Universe will have your back—and serve you right back.

SHELLS

*Shells are beautiful vessels
of ancient wisdom.*

Shells connect me with peace, as they have connotations of flow, water, waves and just being—all things I find very healing. Shell paintings and pictures are calming for our nervous system. Shells remind us to treasure and connect with our oceans, as if we don't live near the sea, we can forget. I like to tune into the sounds within shells to transport myself to the beach. Through shells, we can connect with awe, wonder and gratitude—pondering the beautiful creatures who have left their homes for us to enjoy. I associate shells with feelings of childhood lightness and freedom and carefree seaside days. I visualise walking on sandy shell-filled beaches and at the same time connecting with the ions that radiate from crashing waves.

If we can't visit the ocean regularly as part of our self-care healing and grounding practice, then at least we have shells. Shells are calming, grounding and nurturing to hold in our hands. As with all elements of nature, shells help to awaken our creativity. One cannot help being inspired by the intricate patterns, unique designs and colour arrays of shells. Through shells, we connect with the power of nature, and through this, the power of ourselves.

Shells can be used in a similar way to crystals. Cleanse them, clear them and charge them in the sun or the moonlight, giving them a night under the stars. The spiral patterns of shells are associated with vortexes of energy, like our own spinning chakra energy centres. They can be used on chakras to help balance them. For example, placing them on the heart chakra can be very soothing, bringing back a sense of peace and flow. Shells placed on the third-eye chakra can help to open our vision, intuition, and spiritual insight. Shells have existed since the beginning of time and serve as a reminder to connect with and remember our ancient wisdom.

Shells are often collected just for their beauty—but perhaps we are perceiving their deeper energy, wisdom and healing power, even if unaware of it. Shells help us to connect with the energy and messages within ancient myths and legends featuring the gods and goddesses of the sea. Use shells in your meditation and visualisation practices. Hold a shell in your hand and allow it to take you on a journey under the sea, creating images of mermaids and underwater paradises.

Shells provide some great messages and analogies for life:

- When observing a shell, we can often only see a part of it, but we know and trust there is more. Embrace and trust in the unknown. Look within to discover more. Just because we can't see something, doesn't always mean it's not there.
- Shells are a reminder to embrace our unique individuality. Each shell is structured and made differently, as are we.
- Just be. Let people admire you just as you are.
- Embrace stillness, quietness and presence.
- Shells are an individual combination of attributes: smooth roundness and sharp edges, just like us. We can embrace all our qualities.
- Shells are uniquely beautiful in their own way. There is no competition between them. They exist harmoniously together.
- Shells serve as a reminder of the beauty of nature—the man-made world pales in comparison.

MESSAGE FOR YOUR PATH TO LOVE

Anything from nature elevates our energy. Shells, by their very existence, unique beauty and sea origins, make us feel good. When we feel good, we are connecting with love. Hold one of your favourite shells and connect with its beauty and essence. Have gratitude as you connect with feelings of awe and wonder—these states are great healers and uplifters, transporting us to love.

SELF-CARE IDEA FOR TODAY

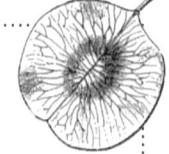

Just as shells leave an imprint on us just by our witnessing them, we have the same effect on those around us. How could you use your power and beauty to positively impact others today?

SNOW

Allow falling snow to dance on your skin and soothe your senses.

An essential part of self-care is generating the healing emotions of gratitude and awe and feeling truly blessed. Snow is like a dusting of blessings on the earth. It is a comforting white blanket. Everything is made pure, refreshed and brand new. Squelching through a perfect canvas of untouched snow elevates our hearts to childlike joy; we smile from the inside out. Snow gives a magical quality to what may have been ordinary. Perhaps it is just our perspective that the earth before the blanketing of beautiful white was ordinary: maybe if we trained our minds to see perfection in everything, our lives (because of our responses to it) would change. Snow falling teaches us to look with fresh eyes; to see what we've been unwilling to see.

Watching snow fall is meditative therapy. It is like an entry, an opening to other realms, as it's often associated with enchanted, fairy-like scenery.

Observing snow, whether it may be in front of us or via images, is magical, cleansing and purifying. Time stands still and expands. It is a doorway to stillness and to the power of the present moment. Creativity and inspiration are stirred.

I felt deep love and a sacred connection to nature as I watched snow fall whilst writing this chapter. Snow is a reminder of the power, majesty and beauty of nature: all qualities that we too can embrace.

Snow reminds us of the impermanence of all things, to appreciate all that is presented before us and to acknowledge that everything passes. Witnessing a snowstorm is captivatingly wondrous, engendering powerful emotion-elevating, loving states. We are privy to the landscape transforming before our eyes. A snap of cold reboots and reinvigorates our senses. We are beings of contrast. We appreciate the warmth far more after a dose of chill and freeze.

MESSAGE FOR YOUR PATH TO LOVE

Gratitude is a quintessential aspect of beautiful self-care. Connect with it next time you get to experience the soothing, magical effects of falling snow. Place a trip to the snow on your bucket list and immerse yourself in its healing majesty.

SELF-CARE IDEA FOR TODAY

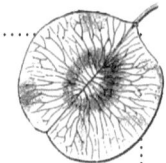

Each snowflake is as unique as you and your needs are. Close your eyes and imagine snow falling around you in a beautiful setting. Reflect on what is unique about you and consider what you may choose next—to feel even more special.

STARGAZING

*Stars remind us that Heaven is always
with us and gazing upon us;
we are never alone.*

Every time we access our power and love, we are engaging in deep self-care. Immerse yourself in the magnitude of the stars to connect with your own infinite light and power. Rejuvenate your spirit and reclaim who you truly are. Allow the stars to sprinkle your soul with light and reignite your divine spark. Be flooded by the grace and beauty of the stars. Allow starlight to infiltrate every cell of your being and shower your energetic body with wisdom, power, and cosmic love. If you star bathe enough, you may be fortunate enough to witness a shooting star and be reminded that your own star can and will rise.

Look to these heavenly bodies and ask to be reminded of your own origins and of the ancient wisdom that resides within you.

What can you remember?

What are you here for?

What soul mission is yours?

Where are your fellow star mates and what possibilities can you unlock together?

Stargazing is an act of love, as we have reverence for the scope and magnitude of the Universe and connect with awe and wonder—elevated states of being. We embrace stillness and presence as we look towards the dazzling displays of diamonds shining above us: a calming act of self-care. Somehow, our day-to-day concerns seem less important when we are intertwined with something so much larger than our earthly existence. We are reminded of our power, as we are an integral part of something so endless and magnificent.

Stars encourage us to connect with the mysteries of life and to embrace the unknown. There is a lot that exists in the stars above us that is unseen and almost unfathomable, but we trust in its existence. We are happy to know that a creative power (beyond our capacity to perceive its glory and totality) is interwoven in the fabric of our existence. We are part of something extraordinary, and therefore *we* must be extraordinary. Use this awareness to dream on a large scale next time you wish upon a star.

Close your eyes and imagine shooting stars traversing the night sky, calling for you to ride on their stardust. In what way can you be a star in your own life? Celebrate your stardom, your successes today—even the smallest twinkles need to be acknowledged to empower you and connect you with your inner worth and love.

The stars are not selective; they shine on us and for all of us. We are all part of the whole and each have a significant role to play; perhaps the stars can help you to unlock the unfolding roles and beautiful destiny that are yours for this lifetime.

Take the time to look above and craft moments to connect with all that is possible for you and our world. Our destiny is woven in the fabric of the stars.

MESSAGE FOR YOUR LOVE TO BLOOM

> Take a moment to gaze out even further beyond the stars and connect with the divine you, that spark of you that resides beyond the heavens, that is larger than this life and also beyond this life. You are safe here, blessed and always protected. This life is but a speck in all of your existence … make it count, and at the same time hold it lightly and reverently, without too much seriousness or significance.

SELF-CARE IDEA FOR TODAY

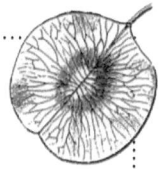

Eagerly anticipate the next star-filled night. Find a cosy blanket and a soft space to lie. Gaze up into the cosmos. Ask the stars to gift to you their ancient wisdom and healing capacity. Allow downloads of unknown potential and gifts to infiltrate your being.

STILLNESS AND PRESENCE

Slowing down, relaxing and being present equals true peace and contentment.

A clear, calm mind allows us to receive messages clairvoyantly and clairaudiently from our higher selves. In stillness we receive our own wisdom and divine guidance. Upon waking, I am extremely clear; sleep has released excessive thinking. This is a magical time when messages and writing come through for me and most likely for you. Sometimes it might be just an image of blessings, like a rainbow, or a powerful message of encouragement or a future desired action. On other occasions, it might be an entire chapter flowing through into my awareness.

I am always in awe of the power and potential within stillness. Stillness creates a vacuum, the space for new thoughts, ideas and inspiration to enter. This book arises from the place of stillness within me. It is where all great works originate from. May you trust in the power of your stillness.

From the power of our stillness, we can enter the unknown and create ourselves anew. We become acquainted with aspects of ourselves that may previously have been obscured. Our ego voice is quietened, and we connect with our higher selves, our intuition and our personal spiritual guidance team. We activate our soothing parasympathetic nervous system and discover our inner field of peace and love.

> 'When you are present in this moment, you break the continuity of your story, of past and future. Then true intelligence arises, and also love ... If your mind is still ... you can sense the peace that emanates from the earth.'
> — Eckhart Tolle

Stillness doesn't have to be formalised through meditation; however, meditation allows us to set aside a personal sacred time for honouring ourselves and our divine connection. We create the space to open to our intuitive gifts, our higher self and the essence of all of life.

Any form of meditation connects us with our heart awareness and the infinite potential of the unknown. If you are an extremely 'busy' person who finds it hard to settle into stillness, guided meditation may be a wonderful tool and practice for you. Making meditation a daily ritual means that stillness is invited to enter our world every day.

Living in present time allows us to manifest more quickly because our energy is with us, and not off in the future or lagging in the past. I continually affirm that my life is where I am in this moment. I live where I am. There is nowhere else I need to be. **Wherever you are, be there, well**. Be free of resisting the present moment and desiring to be someplace else. Affirm, *I am in the perfect place at the perfect time for my highest good*.

Being in stillness allows us to align with love. Gabby Bernstein teaches us that when we are aligned with love, we are super attractors and our alignment sets our manifestations into motion. We can become unstoppable when we align with love and peace. Practise aligning with love through your self-care to perceive powerful, loving energy surrounding you and supporting you always.

MESSAGE FOR YOUR PATH TO LOVE

Slowing down is great self-care, allowing the space to dream and for dreams to come to fruition. In stillness, we become so powerful—we're doing less, and at the same time attracting and manifesting more. Stillness allows us the time and presence to focus on the good in our lives.

Feeling good through self-care connects us with the powerful energy of stillness as we are embracing rather than avoiding the present moment. Be in love with the being that you are becoming and with the power and miraculous wonder within the stillness of the Universe.

SELF-CARE IDEA FOR TODAY

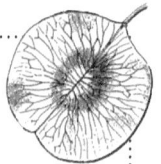

Embrace these affirmations:
- I allow my sense of quiet and peace to exponentialise.
- In stillness, I am aligned with love, drawing in wonder, magic and all that is for my highest good.
- In stillness, I trust that everything is being taken care of by the source of love within me and by the cosmic source that I connect with.
- Through stillness, I quieten the ego agenda and hear my higher guidance.
- In stillness, I can surrender, allowing the Universe to step in with her unique form of guidance and creative potential.

SUNSETS

Sunsets speak to us in the language of love.

I feel honoured to live on planet Earth when I witness the spectacular beauty of a sunset. A beautiful setting sun fills me with immense awe, wonder, gratitude and appreciation in a heartbeat. These feelings are the ultimate in self-care.

There's a stillness, a calm and a connection to all that is love imbued into every cell of my body as the sun shows me her glory at the end of every day. When I've been to places in the world where large groups of people gather to honour this natural event, it feels like a sacred ritual connecting all in attendance. I have hope for all of humanity during these hallowed times.

Through sunsets, we learn the importance and power of observation. We are called to focus and witness reverently what is before us in the moment, for if we allow distraction, the miracle can pass us by.

Sunsets embolden my trust and faith in the power of the Universe, along with its grand plan for us all. Sunsets occur repeatedly; we can trust in this. Each day, we are granted a new beginning, a reset, if we choose.

Sunsets are love in action because they fuel the love within. On a recent island visit, my husband and I cherished the sunsets. As I was loving the sunset, I felt even more love for him. It was a bonding moment over beauty and presence.

With sunsets, no two evenings are the same. In life, no two days are the same. The challenge is to find the beauty within it all. Sunsets can show us the way to step through this door. Beauty seeks and creates beauty.

Colour is healing and uplifting and the magnificent combinations of hues within sunsets are captivating, stilling and calming; we are momentarily taken from our day-to-day existence and truly mesmerised. Sunsets invite in the sacred; they are prayer-like to gaze upon. One time, I was watching the sun set in a state of meditative stillness, when the early evening colours (that appear on the cover of *Pearls of Wisdom: For Your Path to Peace*) spoke directly to me: *Your book is blessed and larger than you are. It will be seen all over the world, expansive and beautiful, just as sunsets are.*

Sunsets allow us to embrace the cyclical nature of life. As the sun goes down each day, we can let go of any darkness, knowing that the light will return very quickly and effortlessly. Just as we can trust that the sun will rise each day, we can trust that there is a new day of hope and possibility presented for us on repeat.

When each day is over, focus on what you have done best, on what you are grateful for, and peacefully let it all go. Trust that you have done enough and are enough, and peacefully anticipate great rewards for your efforts.

Greet each new day with excitement. We get to begin again as the sun rises. We can rise again, again and again.

MESSAGE FOR YOUR PATH TO LOVE

Care for yourself by connecting with the calm and enchantment that nature displays for us in her resplendent evening panoramas. The beauty captured in sunsets activates the love within us and therefore the connection we have to universal love and its accompanying guidance and support.

SELF-CARE IDEA FOR TODAY

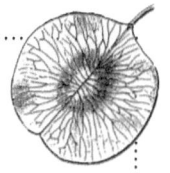

We are given so many opportunities to start anew, to be anew and to create anew. Each day, the slate is wiped clean, and we have a blank canvas to fill. Reflect on each day before sleep and then let it go. Each day the sun rises is vital, as it is another new day in your life.

What will you do with each precious day? What questions can you ask yourself to bring beautiful positive energy and possibility into each new day?

Perhaps it might be:

- What can I do today that I was unwilling or unable to do yesterday?
- What can I do, think, feel or create today that is greater than yesterday?
- What can I let go of as the sun lets go today?

SUPPORT CREW

We receive ourselves more fully through the love of others.

An important part of self-care is having a support team. People to laugh with, cry with and explore life with. Those who can help us access our own wisdom and power. We need support to inspire us, challenge us and help us become the best versions of ourselves. We need friends, colleagues, mentors, animals, lovers, healers and even regular faces we see and chat to at stores to guide us or simply elevate our energy. Our energy creates our life.

Our support team shows up in many guises and many are Earth angels in disguise. Our support crew will often remain the same if we don't change and our life doesn't change. As we evolve, so do our friendships, connections and support crew. Honour the process and the ebb and flow involved. Avoid holding on too tightly to individuals and groups. Allow them to be what they will be and when they will be.

Some people stay in our lives seemingly forever, and others come and go. Trust you are drawing to you who you need, and will love, for each stage of your life. Tracey, my very wise client, says that people come into our lives for a reason, a season or a lifetime.

Our connections teach us, heal us, challenge us and uplift us when we most need it and are therefore an important part of both our self-care and our journey to love. We all seek and thrive through connection—especially those associations infused with love. Give up needing to be needed through fear of others leaving and allow your relationships to evolve to match the next level of you.

Be prepared for life to show you what you need; sometimes that includes times to be your own support team—providing time out from the impact, opinions and intervention of others. We arrive on the planet 'alone' and leave alone. But in truth, we are never truly alone, as our spiritual connections and guidance team are always with us and always waiting for us to reach out and contact them.

In life, we often need to go it alone, especially if we are pioneers treading new ground, venturing where others aren't yet ready to go, or haven't gone before. Sometimes we are called to lead and that can occasionally be lonely or overwhelming as others look to us for so much. Extreme self-care is required during times and scenarios when we are our only support system.

Our hearts long for beautiful, positive connections. Feel, embrace and receive the joy of others in your support team to enhance and allow in more of your own love.

There is an abundance of joy and love for us all. Just because someone is experiencing something doesn't mean we can't too—in our way, in our time, for our highest good. We aren't excluded or rejected—this only occurs via our own judgements, perceptions and reactions. Choose loving thoughts and responses for all your connections: those who are showing up for you as part of your support crew. Focus on who or what is there for you, rather than who or what you have decided you are missing out on. Perhaps those who are frequently 'absent' are not for you and your highest good moving forward.

FOMO (fear of missing out) is the opposite of self-care. It means we have lost trust in ourselves, in our value and in the power we have to attract into our lives who we desire and require—for all the seasons and cycles of our lives. Nature draws to her the nourishment and support she desires, and so can we. We are nature too, and thus have her power and manifesting ability.

MESSAGE FOR YOUR PATH TO LOVE

We inhabit an 'ask and you shall receive' universe when we are connected to love and supported by others, and when we support ourselves through our own self-care. Establish your best possible support situations and crew to foster your greatest potential and connection with love.

SELF-CARE IDEA FOR TODAY

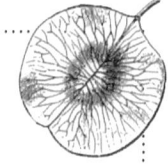

Who or what can support you, your self-care needs and your connection with love this day?

TEA

Teatime is me time.

I really don't know how I survived for decades without discovering the nurturing benefits of teatime. The word tea is now synonymous (for me) with comfort, peace and nurturing, such is the magical power of positive conditioning. I have created teatime as a beautiful ritual: boiling the kettle, selecting today's gorgeous cup or mug, and choosing that moment's tea is a form of meditation for me. I'm absorbed in the process and already in a state of peace before I've sat down in a favourite spot to enjoy my quieting, stilling time for tea. When I choose a little piece of nature heaven in which to enjoy my tea, it is made even more special—the sun on my face, the breeze rustling the leaves, the birdsong and the bees buzzing; there's peace in every cell in my body.

My teatime is simple, powerful self-care; a loving act; the gift of time to take a minute (or many) just for me.

Over time, I have turned teatime into healing time as I've researched the health benefits of herbal teas. I find chamomile tea deeply relaxing, lemongrass and ginger uplifting, peppermint stomach soothing, lemon balm settling for stress and anxiety, rosehip immune-system enhancing, and hibiscus rich in antioxidants. Many teas like chamomile have antiviral and anti-inflammatory properties too. (If you have any existing medical conditions or take medication, it is advisable to check for possible contraindications.) There appears to be a herbal blend for almost every emotional or physical ailment: nature's gift to us and our own personally designed apothecary centre.

Tea brings us back to self-love, as it can become a beautiful honouring of self, a calming ritual. The warmth, the comfort, the hands hugging our favourite cup: self-care activated. Drinking tea provides us with moments to centre, to ground, to breathe, to go within, to come back to oneself, to be still, to contemplate, to connect with one's intuition—providing time to hear the whispers of the Universe.

MESSAGE FOR YOUR PATH TO LOVE

Effortless self-care and uncomplicated doorways to love abound in our day-to-day living. Embrace teatime (or your own equivalent rituals) to achieve quick, powerful moments of self-care and amplified connection to your inner well of love.

SELF-CARE IDEA FOR TODAY

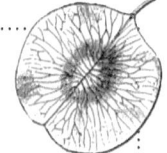

Decide how you would like to feel today. Do your research and find a tea to support that mood and intent.

THE GREAT TRANSITION (HORMONES)

Unravel the hormone mystery to unveil the power and potential of you.

When I was a much younger woman, I would hear women talking about menopause and push it aside as something to ignore until a (much) later time. I wondered what all the fuss was about. I did, however, notice that menopausal women were often unhappy and 'overwhelmed' and we needed to be a little more careful not to upset them in the workplace. In my mind, I thought I would just tick all 'that' off with ease when the time came, and I wouldn't lose my way as many women appeared to be doing. I now know, through my work with many clients and through my own experience, that successfully navigating menopause can be a very fine line, and even a sink-or-swim experience.

I became determined to break all the norms and truly thrive. What I hadn't anticipated was that this life stage was an area fraught with much misinformation, confusion and limited understanding, and at the same time sprinkled with knowledge that was so wonderfully life changing, if one only knew where to find it. Fortunately, there are amazing medical and alternative health therapists out there navigating their way so beautifully and successfully through this minefield of both helpful and hindering information to make this transformation as easy and successful as possible for millions of people—many of whom are in the trenches with this right now, desperately wanting answers and solutions.

I do not have any medical knowledge and would never profess to be any kind of expert. In fact, much of 'medicine' is filled with mystery to me. The wisdom that I do have to offer is all that I have researched and put into practice to assist my own transition into the power years and those of my clients. In sharing what has worked for me, I hope that something may assist you on your journey.

What I have come to realise through discussions with many clients is that we each have a completely unique response and profile in what we experience and what works for us.

The power of people sharing and discussing their experiences and successful approaches to perimenopause and menopause can never be underestimated.

My own foray into this field began in my late forties, where many weird and not-so-wonderful things were happening in my body. This was particularly challenging and stressful as the 'symptoms' changed regularly, so I could never pinpoint anything in particular as 'wrong'. Unfortunately, trips to doctors' surgeries were less than successful and I would often come away even more confused. I began avoiding doctors' surgeries … which I know is not an ideal or responsible choice. The upside of this was that it forced me to take my health into my own hands. I had to embrace preventative care and turn myself, my mind and my body into a healing machine. I researched and trialled many modalities. I studied the work of experts in the field and put into place what I was learning, until I started to feel how I wanted to feel.

It was my choice, my intent, my will, my faith that was proving to be most powerful.

In sharing below what I found to be true for me—my hope is that there may be some approaches that resonate with you or work for you, your body and your life.

A successful transition through menopause requires a complete and utter overhaul on a spiritual, mental, emotional and physical level. It is our greatest stretch, where we can transition and transform into our most beautiful butterfly ever. Can you picture them? We are seeking to become whole; to successfully enter our power years. What is required is self-love in the form of extreme self-care and self-awareness.

Looking back, I have come to realise that PMS can be an early call to address what is going on within. Our inner world is that place many of us avoid looking at unless we are forced to peel back some layers often through a crisis, or a dark night of the soul; where what we have been doing is no longer working to give us the health, wellbeing, peace and contentment that we desire. Each month, our PMS reactions can show us what we need to address on an emotional and mental level. What we do not deal with at these levels can end up finding its way into our physical body, presenting itself as stress, dis-ease, disease and hormonal imbalance, which can then affect how we feel, how we behave and how our bodies function.

I began to study my PMS reactions to learn about me. I started to question me. What was happening this month to make me feel irritated? What needs weren't being met? What was triggering my self-doubt, anxiety, self-judgement, or intolerance of others? What made me feel better? Was I needing to be heard, to express my truth? What forms of self-care did I require? Did I need more exercise or a new kind? Did alternative therapies help? My questioning and actions would vary from month to month, but there was always something to learn.

I believe that if we start doing the 'work' during intense PMS stages, we are far better equipped when the transition stages and demands amp up in perimenopause and menopause. Anything we have not dealt with on a spiritual, mental, emotional and/or physical level rises up to be healed in our transition years. We are meant to get free of all that limits us, to move into our postmenopause power years as the best people we can be—and that means doing what is meaningful and joyful for us and honouring our authentic selves. We are the only ones that have the knowledge of what that is, and we find it within when we've cleared our shadow aspects to the best of our ability.

What a gift we are often presented with through our 'less than ideal' PMS selves. Not all women experience PMS, or perhaps they haven't identified it as such, or they are already doing the inner work. Regardless, we all have work to do on getting free of all that no longer serves us to allow our ascension towards our greatest potential and to enjoy our happiest, most peaceful and productive selves.

For me—to encourage you—my best, most fulfilled, most adventurous, most exciting, most fun, healthiest and most abundant living arrived in my fifties, my power years. Life still presents challenges, but I am powerful enough to handle them all. I am stronger from all that I've lived through and all the adversity I've transmuted into wisdom and strength, as are you.

What I came to know as true for me:

- Our weight matters: it sets us up for hormonal health. Being overweight can lead to insulin resistance and hormonal imbalance. Being underweight—that is, several points under the recommended BMI—affects our body's ability to efficiently store and utilise hormones for optimal health. A healthy weight range sets us up for greater success; we reduce the severity of the 'battle'.

- A healthy body free of toxins, mould, fungi, heavy metals, viruses and unhelpful bacteria has a greater chance of hormonal balance. Viruses gain strength during times of stress and lowered immune function. Two viruses that I battled with, Epstein-Barr and glandular fever, seemed to rear their heads during times when I was run-down or stressed. I found the work of Anthony William (the Medical Medium) most enlightening regarding clearing the body of these hindrances. He believes that much of our menopause symptoms are in fact due to a sluggish liver, which makes sense as, around our fifties, many of our lifestyle choices can be catching up with us. Heal your liver, get healthy, and menopause should pass you by with relative ease. I am a fan of his celery juice protocols.

- Get nutrient levels checked. Nutrient deficiency affects the functioning of all systems in the body, including our hormonal system. Zinc can enhance immunity and libido, two things that hormonal imbalance can upset. I also found herbal supplements and Chinese medicine to be good hormone balancers. Magnesium was great for calming my nervous system.

- Exercise clears stress and reduces inflammation in the body. Yoga and its many styles clear and balance our chakra energy system, which helps to balance us and our hormones.

- Embrace liver and gut health. Eat clean, avoid additives and reduce dairy, gluten, alcohol, caffeine, sugar and any foods that are inflammatory for you. Hormonal balance is optimised through the correct fuel for our bodies and a healthy liver and gut.

- Energy medicine and energy healing clear stress and mental, emotional and spiritual issues from us before they upset the functioning of the body. It is difficult to heal physically if we haven't healed on an energetic level. Anything that assists the optimal functioning of our body assists hormonal balance. Think reiki, acupuncture, kinesiology, and Bach and bush flower remedies. Explore Ayurvedic medicine.

- Seek joy, not stress. Joy is the great healer and balancer—the antithesis of stress. Do what it takes to reduce stress, as the associated adrenal fatigue and high cortisol levels negatively impact our hormones and make us tired. Finding passion and purpose contributes to our joy. What lights us up, lights up every cell in our body. Acknowledge and seek to clear and enhance feelings, and embrace affirmations, meditation, creativity and nature to elevate your (healing) emotions.

- Foster loving connections. Love in our hearts heals our bodies and balances our hormones. Give yourself permission to create distance from people that do not feel good to be around. Our connections should nourish us. They should allow us to feel seen, understood, appreciated and loved. In our menopause years, we have most certainly earned the right to choose who we spend our time with. Go for quality over quantity with friendships. We do not want our friendships to become another form of stress or work—that is, trying to find the time to catch up with hundreds of people, which may take away from precious self-care time.

- Another part of my research that I found particularly interesting was around the benefits of intermittent fasting. It is used to address insulin resistance (lowering insulin levels) and the weight gain connected with our hormone fluctuations. The visceral fat—the most dangerous form, associated with belly weight gain—is targeted through this process. At a very basic level, it involves having an early evening meal and then not eating for around fourteen to sixteen hours. In short, this approach is reputed to allow our insulin levels to stabilise; to allow us to better utilise our fat stores and produce more human growth hormone; and to also allow time for our bodies to process waste. As with anything connected with dietary changes, it is always sensible to seek medical advice if you have underlying health issues. What is a gift to one person's body can be a hindrance to another—such is our unique blueprint.

- Find a wonderful women's health specialist and try hormone therapy or herbal supplementation. If our progesterone is too low or our estrogen too high, we do not feel good, and our bodies do not function optimally. Too much estrogen and we get night sweats, hot flushes and heavy cycles. Progesterone is reported to be anti-inflammatory and essential for hair health, and assists in preventing the nocturnal 2.00 am waking that many women experience with high cortisol levels. Unbalanced hormones can also trigger insulin resistance and autoimmune responses, so we need to find a way to balance them. Getting hormone levels checked regularly is essential before embarking on any hormonal replacement therapy. I will say I briefly tried a very low-dose hormone cream and it made me feel horrendous. I felt like my whole system was gearing up to run a race, but some people find it amazing—that is just further evidence of how all our bodies respond differently. Just keep trying until you find what works for you. We need to embrace trial and error until we find the 'formula' that works best for us.

- Sleep is our ally in all things. It is essential for healing, stress reduction and hormonal balance. Sleep is self-care.

> Getting lots of sleep is not being unproductive or lazy; it is an act of self-love. We require our shutdown time to effectively deal with life and release daily emotions.

I hope from my list of 'successes' that you perceive you can have happy hormones and a happy life. It is all about lifestyle and physical, mental, emotional and spiritual health.

There are so many contributing factors that enhance or detract from our transition experience. For me, it required a complete healing metamorphosis, which coincided with leaving a high-stress teaching career. It was time to rebuild myself. The old me had to make way for the newer, more powerful and loving version of me (that had been waiting in the wings for too long while I was 'busy' taking care of other things).

I changed me, my thinking, my body, my hormones and my life. My body had to become a healing organism, so I had to get out of the way of anything that affected its optimal functioning.

My body and I now have great respect and deep love for each other. We cherish each other and communicate beautifully.

The key is having enough self-love and self-respect to embrace self-care indulgently and relentlessly, particularly through these transition years. We require our best-ever emotional, mental, physical and spiritual health to thrive during these years. We require massive knowledge and a massive toolkit. Be proactive in your research and try, try, try until you succeed.

There is a place for modern medicine and alternative medicine. I did, however, find alternative medicine to be more preventative—picking up emotional, mental, spiritual and physical issues before there was great impact.

A key question moving forward is, *How am I going to take care of me and express love towards me?* This question will allow you to focus on you and your needs, to rise above all that is in the way of your best health and best life. Our hormones are calling to us for balance! It is time, our time. Please give yourself permission.

We deserve the beautiful life and the freedom that awaits us, but we have to do the work. There can be no more sweeping things under the rug or turning a blind eye. Our truthful and most authentic selves will no longer allow it. Listen to the gentle whispers of your body and soul so they do not have to shout to get your attention.

Through my own journey and process towards wellness, I discovered that many underlying health conditions are unwittingly neglected, as we think they are just menopause symptoms. When we are healthy, there are many experts that believe there are very few menopause symptoms. My advice to younger people is to get healthy on all levels before the perimenopause years begin. During this time of transition, all things on all levels surface to be healed so we can enter our power years free and clear and whole.

Our true potential and optimal wellbeing are calling. We deserve these and are worthy.

MESSAGE FOR YOUR PATH TO LOVE

Our transition years require our love and care as we undergo the process of unearthing all that our bodies and spirits don't require moving forward into our power years—with the ultimate goal being peace in mind, peace in body, peace in life. Our transition can be quite a reactive, challenging and intolerant time, as we use so much energy trying to find our way through much change. Be kind to yourself if you feel like withdrawing and hibernating from life at times, as much calm and self-care is required to come out the other side of this process of transformation as our best selves.

SELF-CARE IDEA FOR TODAY

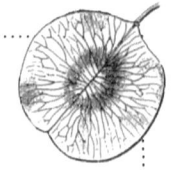

Each person has their own unique experience in the great transition and requires an equally individual approach. Review your self-care. Are you giving yourself the best environment and modus operandi to thrive? What could you trial next? Who could you turn to for advice or support? Take new steps today.

TRUST

Trust allows us to utilise the power of what we believe to dream into existence what we require and desire.

Moving away from fear and into trust is an act of self-care and self-love. Trusting in ourselves, in the unknown and its potential for possibility, and in the life that is unfolding for us, and at the same time having faith in the power of divine guidance is freeing, peaceful and loving.

A lack of trust in ourselves can begin very early in life. It starts when we defer repeatedly (and beyond what is healthy for our evolving potential) to our parents, teachers and other authoritarian figures. We become very familiar with the pattern of 'someone else knows best'. This becomes even more powerful when we are validated for aligning with dominant opinions and approaches, as then we are often deemed good and valuable.

Unfortunately, the pattern of trusting others above ourselves can continue well into our adulthood if we don't develop awareness around this pattern. We can give our power away almost as a conditioned response. We need to reach a place of knowing in our hearts that when we perceive something or feel something in our bodies, then this is our truth.

For too long, we have placed our trust in people, institutions, methodologies and movements outside of ourselves. No one and no thing has more knowledge about us than we have within. You are the leader of the kingdom of you; step fully into your role.

Trust is discerning what is real and true for us and connecting with this despite the white noise of the opinions of others and the fearful voice of our own ego. I have found if it feels light, it is often right. Trusting our inner wisdom takes practice and the deep inner work to know what we are resisting, what is triggering us, what is coming up to be healed and what is really going on. Our emotions and feelings are great teachers if we are willing to sit with them, experience them and recognise and appreciate what is truly occurring within us and for us. Our bodies are great at letting us know what feels heavy and untrue for us.

Our wisdom is within us; we just need to get out of our own way by trusting it. We do this by caring for ourselves, loving ourselves, and knowing we are our own power and authority.

Trust is extremely powerful, as it means we are liberating ourselves from ego dominance and connecting with our higher selves, divine guidance, and our intuition. It means we are open to co-creation; we are not seeking to do things, control things and force things to happen in our way and on our time. We step into flowing with the tides of life, trusting that all is happening for our highest good in divine timing.

Trust is a great act of self-care, as it calms us and allows us to function from our parasympathetic nervous system: the place of receiving, nurturing and connection with the divine feminine. It is the perfect counterbalance for living through the sympathetic nervous system, which is synonymous with doing, acting, forcing, and fight-or-flight modes. Trust allows us to access our greatest peace and calm—true states of love.

Through trust, our beliefs (which create the foundation of our living) become influential creators grounded and centered in love. We know deeply that our beliefs create the experiences that we see forming on the canvas of our lives. This gives us great power to create our own reality, as we take full responsibility for the stories, ideas, attitudes and responses that we allow to influence our life.

Trust in our lives can show up in many diverse and synchronistic ways. It may be that we are experiencing chronic illness and despairing at where to find the best healing and support people to assist us during this turbulent time. When we trust that our bodies and lives are healing us twenty-four seven, the right people, modalities, therapies and information can miraculously show up and invariably take us on the perfect path for our healing to unfold.

When we live in a state of trust, our divine purpose and pathway can reveal itself to us with greater ease and alacrity. We take joy from serving in life and life then serves us in miraculous, wondrous ways.

When we trust ourselves, we no longer need the armour, barriers and fear that separate us from connection, intimacy and receiving. We can open our hearts to greater depths of love and nurturing.

Trust allows us to live in the powerful state of gratitude, as we intrinsically know that life is always conspiring to bring us what is for our highest good. Gratitude is a great catalyst for drawing the decadence, the beauty and the miracles of life towards us at astonishing rates.

As our self-care deepens, our self-love (and our relationship with ourself) deepens, and we trust ourselves and our intuition more freely and effectively. When we don't second-guess ourselves, life can deliver to us what we desire and also what we require for our highest good. We trust that all is well, and our path is guided. We embrace trust one step at a time through each moment of self-care, self-love and self-honour. Trusting ourselves allows us to take the plunge and look within to see what we need to release in order to evolve and utilise the gifts we've been given.

Loving yourself connects you with the magic of you and aligns you with your path, peace, potential and purpose. Love yourself and you can trust that what life is presenting for you and calling for you is perfectly designed for you. Everything we experience teaches us something about ourselves, increasing our self-trust. The more we know and understand ourselves, the greater our awareness is. Our awareness raises our self-worth, which in turn heightens our self-love and the trust we have in ourselves. It is a circular, interconnected process.

Trust is a lifetime journey requiring patience and compassion for all that we are, for all that we've learned (through our challenges, mistakes, transgressions and triumphs) and for all that we are becoming.

MESSAGE FOR YOUR LOVE TO BLOOM

> Love yourself enough to trust yourself. Trust in the seeds you are planting. Give your creations time to grow. Trust allows for change. The combined power of your trust and love has the potential to unleash wonderful things in this world. Trust and back yourself and your decisions. Have great faith in the way your life is unfolding.

SELF-CARE IDEA FOR TODAY

Ensure your beliefs are supporting your ability to trust. Some of the most dominant and powerful beliefs I like to foster around trust are:
- My life unfolds as one blissful experience to the next ... and the next
- There is a constant loving energy that moves through me and all around me, taking care of everything on my behalf
- Miracles, awe and wonder abound
- My life is divinely guided and inspired
- My divine purpose unfolds every second of every day

What beliefs around trust are you choosing (and ultimately seeing) in your life? Rewrite these beliefs today if they are not originating from a place of love. Change your beliefs, change your life. Yes, you are that powerful!

TRUTH

The truth is everything. You stand in your light when you stand in your truth.

The truth will set you free. What does this truly mean?

I feel it means that we are seeing, owning, acknowledging and accepting all aspects of ourselves without judgement. Judgement is anti-self-care and anti-love. When we are willing to see the whole truth of ourselves and love ourselves regardless, then we are free. We are free to be ourselves and to express this in a plethora of unique and authentic ways. We don't have to people please or make excuses for ourselves. We have strong boundaries because we know who we are and what we require to live our best lives. It means our self-worth is strong and we are functioning from a space of love and contributing to our wellbeing.

The truth awakens and sets us free, as we cannot change or heal what we are unable to acknowledge. Connect with your inner guidance and allow your truth to be divinely guided, powerful and for the highest good of you and possibly others. Listen to your higher self to weaken the machinations of the ego—you have put it on notice; it is no longer in control.

Speaking our truth is caring for ourselves, our opinions, our feelings and our authenticity. Connecting with our truth brings us peace, as we are not hiding from what is true. Lying to ourselves or others arises from a place of fear. Truth elevates our love as we hold ourselves in high esteem.

If we are truthful with ourselves, we will be more likely to be truthful with others. We will effectively communicate our thoughts, feelings and emotions, and in so doing create the conditions for optimal mental and emotional health. We aren't holding back aspects of our own being and have the freedom to create and live our own reality.

Living from a place of truth inspires others to do the same. Truth is a wonderful contagion. Just imagine a world steeped in truth as opposed to deception. All things would have the chance to move to the light, to love.

Make choices that reflect and are in alignment with your truth. Trust in your truth and express it. Feel your truth in your body and in your heart. Be authentic in your life and let go of people who don't resonate with your truth or would judge you for it. Allow each person to have and be their truth with freedom.

Being really honest with ourselves allows for deep healing and deep love, as we are not denying what needs to be acknowledged and released—from this space, we are proactive and at our most powerful. Develop your power of X-ray vision; be willing to truly see yourself, your stuff and the motivations of others.

Avoid becoming involved in debate, as it doesn't take anyone closer to their truth. Release the need to fight or align. We do not have to justify, validate or recruit support for what we feel or believe, even if we feel strongly that we are right.

If your point of view is not well received, and someone is not willing to explore a greater truth, let it be—that is, avoid taking the energetic hook of needing to be right or to dominate the conversation. All we need to do is honour our own truth, which is loving and honouring ourselves. We can feel what we feel without needing validation from others.

MESSAGE FOR YOUR LOVE TO BLOOM

Speaking our truth is essential for nurturing our love. This is a peaceful, caring and loving stance for us to take with ourselves. Honouring our truth sends a deep message to our psyche that we are worthwhile; that what we have to say is important. Expressing our truth is vital for our wellbeing, particularly when we do not need to recruit others for validation or agreeance. Our self-care encourages us to stand in our integrity and make choices that are in alignment with our highest good, and our love.

SELF-CARE IDEA FOR TODAY

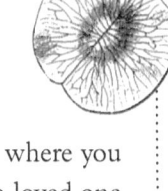

Sit quietly and think of somewhere in your life where you are holding back your truth. This may be with a loved one or a colleague. Breathe deeply, centre yourself and calmly express yourself. Do this without any form of aggression, or risk losing respect for self and from others. We give away our power and are not heard when assertion rolls into aggression.

WEDDINGS AND EVENTS

Special occasions invite more of us to love and celebrate.

If you're anything like me, black tie and formal functions are not part of your day-to-day existence. These occasions fall more naturally into the category of miracle occurrences. So, like any miracle, I treat them with great regard and appreciation when they arrive. Special celebrations are beautiful opportunities for self-care in disguise—as through them, we celebrate life and in so doing celebrate us.

When attending special events, I am both captivated and uplifted, as there is much elevated energy associated with such occasions. People have gone to the trouble of making themselves feel and look wonderful. They have stepped out of the everyday and into the magical unknown, where surprises, possibility and miracles abound. Unless you are the organiser of the event, no one truly knows what will unfold. There is often a mix of nervous excitement before attending—we know we are alive! We are present in the power of the moment.

The elevated energy that prevails at weddings and black-tie events is contagious, as one soaks up the beautiful outfits, hair, make-up and joy amongst those fortunate enough to attend. People are generally feeling good, willing to be complimentary to others and putting the best versions of themselves forward—high vibe, love-inducing states.

The venues and rooms holding these events are meticulously put together, demonstrating love and care in action. Soak up the beauty of the flowers, the romantic lighting, the carefully chosen music and the decadent table settings to fuel your own inner well of light and love. Be in a state of gratitude for the opportunity to be at such an event to further enhance elevated emotions. Enjoy being cared for as amazing waitstaff serve you culinary delights and drinks in elegant glasses. Enjoy being a prince or princess for the night. You are worth it; you deserve it. And who knows? By being in such an appreciative state, you may draw more of these wondrous occasions into your world—and the outfits to take you to them in the most beautiful style. We are all worthy of a Cinderella ball moment (minus any losing-our-shoe drama). We may feel so good we even draw in our prince, long before midnight.

MESSAGE FOR YOUR PATH TO LOVE

Self-care and love exist in elevated emotional states. The next time you are at a wedding, absorb the love of a new bride and groom to reconnect with feelings of love. Use these feelings to send a powerful message out into the Universe asking how you may receive more love in your life from this moment on.

SELF-CARE IDEA FOR TODAY

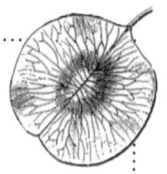

Don't wait for an invite. Start dreaming of your own formal occasion and plan it. It does not have to be for an especially significant milestone or celebration. We are alive; all days are significant. Your planned event could just be for fun, to celebrate you, to embrace some long-overdue decadence and hedonism. It doesn't have to be about the number of invites; sometimes a party of two can be just as memorable.

WITNESSING SUFFERING

Our potential is drawn from us, for us, through adversity.

Through an ongoing commitment to self-care and my own learning process, the growth in my wisdom and strength has generally enabled me to navigate my way through instances of personal suffering with reasonable success. However, what still challenges me greatly is witnessing and then experiencing the suffering of a loved one. This I find more challenging and taxing, physically and emotionally, than my own duress. If I don't stay aware, I can descend into empath overload with unfortunate ease. My empath abilities require that I maintain my energetic boundaries, trust in the journey of another, and work on knowing where someone else's emotions end and mine begin.

The pain of a loved one can evoke feelings of despair and powerlessness. I often feel a sense of hopelessness at my inability to transform another's suffering into wisdom and peace in a heartbeat. It can feel like I am in the throes of an extreme emotional hangover, as part of me is both consciously and unconsciously attempting to take on and remove suffering for another. I must catch myself and remind myself that denying someone of their suffering could deny them access to new directions, new thinking and their greatest potential.

These types of experiences challenge me to my very core, teaching me so much about myself and how life works best for the highest good of all. Effectively witnessing the suffering of loved ones requires many seeds of self-care for my love to bloom enough to support me in being there for another, without taking on what is not mine to take.

I realise through these heart-wrenching encounters that I do not get to 'play God'. I can't change or heal that which is not mine to change or heal. I am not and nor should I be in control of anything for another. I can only manage my own reactions and dive into my self-care toolkit to avoid toxic worry that I do not want to flow on to a loved one. I can also catch any ego dramatising, which encourages me to go over and over an issue with useless thinking. I know that all I can really do is provide support as requested. I can also be totally present with another, giving my best listening ears and the most powerful version of me as a sounding board. From here, I more effectively assist my loved ones to access the inner guidance and wisdom that is wanting to surface through the experience just for them.

My cup must be full first for me to assist another through whatever processing and transmutation of pain they require. I lean into the space of empathy as opposed to sympathy to avoid compromising another's personal power and ability to come out of a situation with grace, wisdom and dignity.

I find the mantra *This too shall pass* to be most helpful. I remind myself that every person is on a healing journey from the moment they arrive on the planet until the moment they leave, and that the most challenging situations bring forth the most growth and wisdom. I remember that my loved ones are stronger than I have any true perception of—and it is not my job to rob anyone of their own growth by attempting to take on and remove their suffering. This is very challenging and very complex 'work' for an empath, as we automatically feel the pain of another and seek to transmute suffering.

The word TRUST is my most powerful ally when witnessing the pain of another. There are no mistakes, only opportunities for growth and detours in new directions. I trust that all is well and that there is a divine plan unfolding that is supporting the individual's healing and the process of awakening to become more of who they are. I trust they have their own spiritual guidance and support team, and that those who 'sign up' for lessons with an element of suffering attached are here to achieve great things. I remind myself of the personal greatness, changes in life trajectory and deep wisdom that I have accessed via adversity.

I seek to understand on some level what may be occurring for another by talking with them and connecting with my own guidance. Too much emotion disconnects me from the strength of my inner wisdom, so I need to breathe and soothe with lots of self-care to be most effective. Stopping the 'fearful thought, fearful emotion' cycle is essential and takes great mind control. Each fearful thought feeds a corresponding fearful emotion, and the loop continues until we take the reins of it and redirect the situation one thought at a time. When fearful emotions that infiltrate every cell in the body take over, there is only one port of call that works: love. I ask to shine every ounce of love that I can rally into the situation and at the same time focus the energy of love directly into the area of my body where I most feel the impact of fearful emotions.

Journalling with the dominant question *What's right about this I'm not getting?* is a most helpful tool. It brings clarity that I cannot access from an emotionally charged narrative. It helps me to honour the person's suffering as a way for them to grow and transform.

I observe regularly what arises for clients out of pain, and I need to remind myself that my loved ones are allowed to have these experiences, if that is what their soul requires.

Along with self-care to help me to be most effective in these situations, connecting with love is my super strength. I can do this quickly through meditation and connecting with nature. Salt baths and energy healing are great for releasing stuck emotions and energies and moving us back to love and peace, where we are most effective in all that life presents: providing a great reset to see difficult situations from a new perspective.

I ask myself, what would love do here? Oftentimes, the answer is do nothing, and step back so others can step up and surrender to something greater as they access their own guidance.

Some affirmations that are particularly helpful for me when dealing with the suffering of another are:

- I focus on the love that surrounds [person's name] and I expect miracles
- I breathe in divine light and love, and breathe out everything that is not
- I return all this to sender with love and conscious awareness
- This too shall pass and quickly
- I connect with the soothing power of my love to heal this
- I shine love on this [epicentre of the body area experiencing the suffering] and transmute the hurt into something beyond my wildest dreams

Questions are also great for opening up to new energies and possible solutions.

Some of my favourite questions for assisting with the process of witnessing the hurt and suffering of loved ones are:

- What would it take for [name of person] to receive some lovely or encouraging news around this situation?
- What would it take for [name of person] to access the lesson or wisdom presented in this scenario with the greatest of ease and in the shortest possible timeframe?
- What would it take for the perfect guidance and support

to show up for [name of person]?
- What beautiful change and transformation can arise from this situation with …?
- In what ways can this suffering be replaced with love, laughter and joy?
- What miracles can [name of person] receive today?
- How can I help [name of person] to see the silver lining and potential for growth in all of this?
- How can I facilitate [name of person] to lighten up to receive the wisdom inherent in this experience?

After asking *What's right about this I'm not getting?* for a particularly troubling scenario I was facing, I was gifted some beautiful imagery and insight.

I saw a road sign pointing to ancient Troy. Next emerged an image of the Trojan Horse. Then the words, 'There is great treasure inside waiting to be unleashed'. This reminded me of the inherent strength of the person whose struggle I was witnessing. What emerged from the Trojan Horse, according to legend, was so powerful and crafty that it could take over a previously impenetrable city of riches.

This was a beautiful reminder for me to step back and trust and let forces greater than me allow situations to unfold as they were destined for the highest good of those involved.

The final stage for me in witnessing suffering is acceptance. Accepting what is and knowing what I can change and cannot. All I can really change is my responses.

Acceptance flows more quickly when I can step into gratitude and appreciation around all that is right, good and working.

Soothing myself requires one attitude and one thought change at a time, leading me back to love and elevated, nurturing emotions.

MESSAGE FOR YOUR LOVE TO BLOOM

For our own sanity and wellbeing, we need to give ourselves permission to push back the pain and suffering of our loved ones (and the world) and stay in our own lane, or in our own bubble—depending on what we require. We can then connect back to our own love.
Refusing to take on the experience of others can sometimes be the greatest, most essential form of self-care. Avoid using the urge to fix or save others as a distraction for connecting with your own inner guidance and doorway to love.

SELF-CARE IDEA FOR TODAY

Surround a loved one who is facing difficulty of some kind in love. Open your heart, build the love within, and imagine this flowing outward to the desired recipient's heart. You will both elevate and receive greater love, peace, and possibility for transmuting pain into awareness.

WORLDS WITHIN THE SAME WORLD

Diversity is the new spice of life.

Within our world, many of us experience different worlds. We need to be okay with knowing that our version of reality and the way we live is going to be largely different to that of many we are closely connected with. We can honour another's world, even if we can't understand or relate to it. Many times, I have had to answer my thinking around *Why would they do that* or *choose that* or *be that?* with *Because they can* or *Because they are doing the best they can with the awareness and tools that they currently possess.* Compassion, love, non-judgement and allowance are key.

I adopt the stance of *My world is not better than anyone else's, just different*, as we are here to learn vastly different things through the tapestry of our lives.

It is futile to compare our world to the world of another. Occupy the world that is orbiting just for you, as it is designed perfectly for you. The great thing is, you are the only one powerful enough to change your world.

Each person's 'world' and experiences are created by their own mental constructs, viewpoints, and thoughts; what they are willing to see and receive; and their general attitudes towards life. The stories we tell ourselves on repeat become our beliefs and these in turn become our reality. What we proclaim goes out into the world like a beacon, often returning to us in some form, such is the powerful nature of words and thoughts. An example of this is when a friend proclaimed, 'There are never any dresses in David Jones that I like, and I can never find a dress for any occasion that I look for!' I, on the other hand, would go in and be surrounded by beautiful dresses. This is because my point of view is that there are just so many beautiful dresses to choose from ... and which ones will I leave behind? Same planet, different world.

We hear these types of proclamations all the time. For example, 'The people in this town are awful', 'Good things happen to other people, never to me', 'I'm unlucky in love', 'Everything I eat goes straight to my hips', 'I am always tired', 'There are no jobs suiting my qualifications' ... and that's what shows up. Then there is the alternate reality: people are just so kind in that town, the service in that restaurant is always amazing, the right friend/job/experience shows up for me just as I need them/it ... and that is what shows up. Once again; same planet, different world.

We each co-create our own reality based on our personal view of the world; how much we are in the grips of the ego; our thoughts, beliefs and personal stories; our connection with divine source; how well we listen and act on guidance; the strength of our self-care regime; and how much we have stepped into claiming our power, love and natural aptitudes. No two worlds will be the same for any of us. **Choose the greatest world to live in for you.**

If you are choosing to create heaven on Earth, yet those around you seem to be choosing the other end of the scale—that is your choice and that is their choice. It is a free-will universe; honour the world you choose to live within. Do not go into the world of another if it is not to your liking, for any reason.

MESSAGE FOR YOUR LOVE TO FLOURISH

Feel bold, blessed and beautiful within your world as you've created it. Know deeply that you have the power to change anything you don't like about your world through the power of your love. Stand in your light and shine so brightly that you may shift some of the darkness from the many worlds around you.

SELF-CARE IDEA FOR TODAY

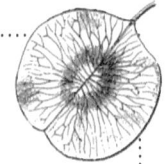

Use your power and love to proclaim your new, upgraded world into existence.
Visualise what it may be like. What does it feel like to be king or queen of this world? Write down your description and come back to it to determine how well you are manifesting your new world into existence.

MY PERSONAL LOVE, CARE AND HAPPINESS MANIFESTO:

A gift from my heart to yours

The key to feeling good and feeling love is to stop feeling all the opposites of it; we know what they are, as we are all too familiar with them. We need to know in our hearts that we can feel good and are worthy of it. Feeling good and feeling love takes one thought, one attitude shift, one action at a time. It is about gently and consistently clearing away all that is in the way of feeling good and feeling love.

We program ourselves to function with so much negativity through our repeated worry, fear and doubt. We need to actually give ourselves permission to feel good and to then commit to it with much verve.

Many of us are afraid to feel good, as we fear it won't last and then we will feel worse. We need to build our worth and confidence from ground zero, if that's what it takes.

We can unlearn all that we thought was real about ourselves and life that in fact was not real—much of this we picked up long before our adult years. We need to stop listening to the ego and connect with our higher self and its messages of love, support and guidance.

Take charge of your mind and you will take charge of your life.

We can choose to stop living in the past, as that's where depression arises, and at the same time avoid jumping into the future, as that's where anxiety is born. Stay in this moment, as this is where our power, peace and potential live. Take care of today and your future will be taken care of before you arrive.

Stay in your own lane and don't compare yourselves to others:

they have their own journey, just as you do. Remove judgement from your existence: it's a nasty little beast that will regularly nip away at your happiness.

Sensitive people are going to feel the unrest of those around them and even the collective: we need to protect and ground our energies regularly and establish strong boundaries. We require extreme self-care to heal, love, bloom and be radiant beacons of healing and love for others.

Our self-care connects us with all that is good within us and around us on all levels: spiritually, emotionally, mentally, physically and energetically. Our bodies, minds and hearts require the correct fuel for heightened wellness. Get free of addictions: they numb us and keep us in the same space and time for way too long. We are and can be so much more when we emerge from addiction. Find your own light and love, and you won't crave things from the outside world to fill any void. We need to move and nurture our beautiful, extremely intelligent, self-regulating and healing bodies for optimal health. Our souls require regular adventures and changes of scenery to reset and inspire. Meditation will, over time, heal your mind and give you access to all of you.

Allow Mother Earth to hold you in her arms and heal you and reveal to you your magic and beauty. Stay alert for signs, synchronicities and miracles: true gifts of love in action. Follow what lights you up, for it will lead you where you need to go for meaning, purpose, creativity and inspiration. Be immersed in the unconditional love of pets. Be all of who you are: your wisest and most loving, powerful and authentic self—there's no need to play small to make others feel better around you. Find someone or several someones to journey through life with who love you as much as you love them. Love yourself enough to give yourself what would make you happy.

The more we honour ourselves, the more freely we will gift our love and the greatest versions of ourselves to others.

THE EFFECTS AND EVIDENCE OF YOUR LOVE IN BLOOM

As love through our self-care penetrates every cell of our being and infuses our life with its power and presence, it can become so innate that we forget to recognise our love in bloom and in action. It is important to stop and reflect on just how amazing we are when we choose to create love within ourselves: a love that influences and infiltrates all those around us.

Our peace, our wisdom, and our choice to embrace self-care and love move those we connect with closer to their own versions of these states. When we embrace love, we energetically give others an invitation and permission to do the same.

The more I care for me, the more love I generate within and the more I write. The more I write, the more I contribute to you and others in the world who are moved by my words.

What is your equivalent? What 'more' of you is revealed to you and others when you allow your self-care to ignite your love?

If you answer yes to at least one of the following questions, you have evidence that your love is in bloom (and cause for celebration).

- Do you feel more positively about your life and purpose?

- Do you feel greater motivation to contribute, to serve in some way to make a difference in the lives of others?
- Are you kinder and more compassionate towards yourself and others?
- Do you wake up most mornings with enthusiasm for what the day may present?
- Do you feel more desire to reach out and connect with others?
- Are your relationships deepening and revealing greater levels of trust and intimacy?
- Are you noticing the beauty all around you?
- Are you beginning to feel a sense of oneness with all of Earth and its occupants?
- Does nature and all its various elements bring you greater peace and joy?
- Do you take greater pleasure in inspiring and uplifting others?
- Is life becoming more magical, surprising and fun for you?
- Are you connecting more fully with your intuition, your inner guide and your wisdom?
- Are you perceiving the miracles, coincidences and synchronicities in your life?
- Are you wishing to pass on your blessings to others?
- Are you able to deflect negativity around you with greater ease?
- Are you able to express yourself more confidently and calmly?
- Has your ability to communicate with others at a deeper level developed?
- Are you starting to see that all your contributions, no matter how seemingly small, have an impact?
- Is peace becoming your natural default system?

- Are you experiencing more contentment in your days?
- Are you finding that new people are drawn to you and your increasing light?
- Are you able to contribute and serve without the need for validation, reward or acknowledgement—and at the same time receive these as wonderful gifts if they are forthcoming?
- Are you sensing the change in others over time just through your presence?
- Are your wisdom and self-worth increasing—do you understand and acknowledge more of you?
- Are people thanking you for the contribution, the impact you are having on their lives?
- Are you developing more tolerance and understanding for the more difficult, painful and downright 'disturbed' individuals who cross your path? Can you see their light even if it is somewhat obscured?
- Can you see the qualities of others reflected in you as mirrors into your own soul?
- Do you have the awareness that we are all part of the human condition and trying to find our own way back to love?
- Are you more patient with your children and listening more intently, making them feel cherished and heard?
- Do you take more time to pet the animals in your life?
- Do you smile at and uplift those you wouldn't normally bother with?
- Are you connecting more beautifully and intimately with your partner?
- Do you value the contributions you are making through your work with increased fervour?
- Are you experiencing greater depths of gratitude and appreciation for the people in your life?

- Do you find yourself judging yourself and others less often?
- Have your feelings of sweet peace helped to harmonise your working relationships?

Check in frequently with these questions to acknowledge your gains in love. Each week, select one or two to keep in mind over a few days to develop. It may be as simple to begin with as expressing gratitude for things, people and situations that may have previously gone unnoticed by you.

Each choice towards your care and love creates ripples of love that touch others in ways often unknown to us. Each time we raise our vibration of love, it energetically connects with and elevates those around us. Your love has a greater reach than you can imagine. Fuel it daily with your self-care.

AFTERWORD

I am in awe and honoured to be the messenger for this work to flow into the world. The choice you have made to read this book is a powerful one. Our self-care is more potently influential than we often acknowledge. Each time we heal, grow, or let go of an unhealthy pattern or behaviour, or gain freedom from a limiting story about ourselves or others, we open to more love, and this love spills forth to others in ways we often don't realise. You are monumentally enhancing your own life, the lives of those around you and the consciousness of the planet, as we are all interconnected.

In prioritising care for yourself, you are caring for your world, our world. You are a miracle worker.

> *'When you care for yourself from a heart-centred, healthy place, you are also caring for the whole of humanity.'*
> — Colette Baron-Reid

Making our personal wellbeing our most important life asset draws more of what we love into our world, effortlessly. A superwoman or superman needs super self-care for super love. Your commitment to advancing yourself through opening your heart to love—by witnessing it all around you and within you—has an impact beyond what you can imagine, as your heart emits a powerful energy that radiates to others. Heart energy is truth beyond words, and the truth sets us free to reveal more of ourselves.

In seeking the path to love, you are allowing the revelation that love abounds all around you to permeate every cell of your body and being. Through this state, you are connecting with the seemingly ordinary, which is in truth the extraordinary. Every time we connect with what feels extraordinary to us, we are connecting with the divine field of energy from which we all originate. We find love through connection and the more things we can connect with, such as those mentioned in my seeds of self-care, the more we get to love. Each act of self-care—along with the perception of the wonder, awe, bounty and beauty that proliferates on planet Earth—connects us with love.

I hope you have learned to look and connect with the wonder of our world and to use this wonder to heal you. Let's look at what is in front of us, what is presenting just for us. Notice and pay attention. Through living this way, peace, happiness and love become our predominant life themes.

Our most powerful and life-changing act of love is deeply caring for ourselves spiritually, emotionally, mentally and physically. I've come to realise through the unfolding of me, thanks to my self-care, just how special I am. I know you will perceive this within you as well—with the understanding that you are no more special than anyone else, and nor do you have to be, as being ourselves is always good enough.

Who we BE, and not what we do, is what defines us. Ultimately, the gift of us is what we bestow in life and for life. We are all seeds of magnificence waiting to bloom—and bloom well we shall through carving our own unique path to love. You have always had these seeds within you, waiting for you.

I thank you wholeheartedly for being you, for contributing to changing the world and for taking this journey with me. I cherish in advance the joy, fulfilment and astonishment that will be yours when you witness the power of love as it flourishes all around you.

The path to love is both highly challenging and exhilarating.

We conquer lots within us, to be free to love.

Congratulations on being an advanced, brave soul who is a part of the pioneering of a new age. Let a beautiful new dawn light up your days.

Much love and care,
Jane x

ACKNOWLEDGEMENTS

Thank you—

Pete, for being beyond imaginable as a husband and for lighting me and my life up in immeasurable ways, every day. Thank you for all the love that you have awakened and inspired within me. I know I've done something very right this lifetime to have drawn you into it, to share it with me. What a team we make.

Dr Barbara Angelas, for helping me to perceive, feel and uncover my true nature, which is love.

Dr Judith Orloff, for insights into the power of making self-care a priority.

Rebecca Campbell, for answering your calling and in so doing helping me to remember who I am, and what I'm here for. Thank you for assisting me to remember the healing power of our connection with nature.

Denise Linn—somehow your work soothes and uplifts me and at the same time encourages my belief around the work I am doing.

My daughter, Julia, for sharing her thoughts around the powerful nature of having pets in our lives as part of our self-care. Her magical relationships with animals have inspired me to elevate my own connections with the animal kingdom.

Kyle Gray, for the high vibes that you create in the world. I have very much enjoyed your words of inspiration.

To my Reiki One Jane Holman Facebook followers, for your support. It has been encouraging beyond words. I am grateful for every like and every share. I am in awe of the countless countries and faraway towns from which you all originate. You have significantly assisted the sharing of my work and its message.

To my readers of *Pearls of Wisdom: For Your Path to Peace*. The beautiful feedback filled my heart and fuelled my desire to allow more writing to come through me, to you. Much gratitude.

My guidance team: you never cease to amaze me with how you work with me, and guide me, and help me to get out of my own way—always leading me back to love.

ABOUT THE AUTHOR

Jane Holman is a former primary school teacher who finished her teaching career to expand her love of writing and energy healing. Through her business, Reiki One, Jane conducts energy healing, intuitive counselling and life coaching whilst providing considerate direction and genuine motivation for aspiring writers. She enjoys assisting people with their inner journeys towards wisdom, peace, love, power, and potential.

Jane lives on the north-west coast of Tasmania. Her second book, *Seeds of Self-Care: For Love and Serenity*, flows gracefully and powerfully on from her first book, *Pearls of Wisdom: For Your Path to Peace*.

www.ingramcontent.com/pod-product-compliance
Lightning Source LLC
Chambersburg PA
CBHW030252010526
44107CB00053B/1671